D1615510

# Glacial Times

**HEALTH SCIENCES LIBRARY, BROOKFIELD**
COLÁISTE NA HOLLSCOILE CORCAIGH

Níl sé ceaduithe an leabhar seo a choimead thar an dáta is déanaí atá luaite thíos.

**This book must be returned not later than the last date stamped below.**

In C                                                                    k as
a ps                                                                    d in
insti                                                                   eful
sum

L                                                                       rary
sour                                                                    ook
brin                                                                    y of
psyc                                                                    ical
que

- T
- T
- T
- T
- P
- T

Thi                                                                     with
psyc

**Sal**                                                                 eatre
*of L*

Forms to be typed or written in block capitals. 1802835

| U.C.C. Library | BOOK PROPOSAL FORM |
|---|---|

Author Surname: RESNIK

Author Forename(s): S

Title: GLACIAL TIMES: A JOURNEY THROUGH THE WORLD OF MADNESS

Place of Publication: 

Publisher: Routledge

Year of Publication: 2005

ISBN (see over): 1583917179

No. of Copies: 3

Price per copy: £18·99

Volume:

Remarks (see over)

Edition:

Proposer: AINE O DONOVAN

Dept.: NURSING

Extn. No.: 1489

Signature of Head of Dept. or Library Rep.

Please tick appropriate box:
2 week loan   short loan   desk reserve

Date Proposed: 18.4.06

UNIVERSITY COLLEGE Library CORK

# THE NEW LIBRARY OF PSYCHOANALYSIS
General Editor Dana Birksted-Breen

The New Library of Psychoanalysis was launched in 1987 in association with the Institute of Psychoanalysis, London. It took over from the International Psychoanalytical Library, which published many of the early translations of the works of Freud and the writings of most of the leading British and continental psychoanalysts.

The purpose of the New Library of Psychoanalysis is to facilitate a greater and more widespread appreciation of psychoanalysis and to provide a forum for increasing mutual understanding between psychoanalysts and those working in other disciplines such as the social sciences, medicine, philosophy, history, linguistics, literature and the arts. It aims to represent different trends both in British psychoanalysis and in psychoanalysis generally. The New Library of Psychoanalysis is well placed to make available to the English-speaking world psychoanalytic writings from other European countries and to increase the interchange of ideas between British and American psychoanalysts.

The Institute, together with the British Psycho-Analytical Society, runs a low-fee psychoanalytic clinic, organizes lectures and scientific events concerned with psychoanalysis and publishes the *International Journal of Psychoanalysis*. It also runs the only UK training course in psychoanalysis that leads to membership of the International Psychoanalytical Association – the body that preserves internationally agreed standards of training, of professional entry and of professional ethics and practice for psychoanalysis as initiated and developed by Sigmund Freud. Distinguished members of the Institute have included Michael Balint, Wilfred Bion, Ronald Fairbairn, Anna Freud, Ernest Jones, Melanie Klein, John Rickman and Donald Winnicott.

Previous General Editors include David Tuckett, Elizabeth Spillius and Susan Budd. Previous and current Members of the Advisory Board include Christopher Bollas, Ronald Britton, Donald Campbell, Stephen Grosz, John Keene, Eglé Laufer, Juliet Mitchell, Michael Parsons, Rosine Jozef Perelberg, David Taylor, Mary Target, Catalina Bronstein, Sara Flanders and Richard Rusbridger.

# ALSO IN THIS SERIES

HS 616·89 RESN

# THE NEW LIBRARY OF PSYCHOANALYSIS

General Editor: Dana Birksted–Breen

HEALTH SCIENCES BROOKFIELD LIBRARY CORK

# Glacial Times

A Journey through the World of Madness

Salomon Resnik

Translated by David Alcorn

Routledge
Taylor & Francis Group

LONDON AND NEW YORK

1696465836

First published 2005
by Routledge
27 Church Road, Hove, East Sussex BN3 2FA

Simultaneously published in the USA and Canada
by Routledge
270 Madison Avenue, New York NY 10016

*Routledge is an imprint of the Taylor & Francis Group*

© 2005 Salomon Resnik

Translation © David Alcorn

Typeset in Bembo by
Keystroke, Jacaranda Lodge, Wolverhampton
Printed and bound in Great Britain by
TJ International Ltd, Padstow, Cornwall

All rights reserved. No part of this book may be reprinted or
reproduced or utilised in any form or by any electronic, mechanical, or other
means, now known or hereafter invented, including photocopying and
recording, or in any information storage or retrieval system, without
permission in writing from the publishers.

This publication has been produced with paper manufactured to strict
environmental standards and with pulp derived from sustainable forests.

*British Library Cataloguing in Publication Data*
A catalogue record for this book is available from the British Library

*Library of Congress Cataloging-in-Publication Data*
Resnik, Salomon.
[Temps des glaciations. English]
Glacial times : a journey through the world of madness / Salomon
Resnik ; translated by David Alcorn.
p. cm.
Includes bibliographical references and index.
ISBN 1-58391-716-0 (hbk.) — ISBN 1-58391-717-9 (pbk.)
1. Psychoses. 2. Psychoanalysis. 3. Body language. I. Title.
RC512.R47313 2005
616.89—dc22
2004025925

ISBN 1-58391-716-0 (hbk)
ISBN 1-58391-717-9 (pbk)

# Contents

# Preface

According to Bion, the physical act of writing provides support for creative thinking. I too need to devote a few hours each day to think about my thoughts and to write up my daily experience. In the Introduction to his *Critique of Pure Reason*, Kant (1963 [1896]: 41) says: 'There can be no doubt that all our knowledge begins with experience.' The faculty of cognition is revealed through the expression of our senses, and, with their help, representations are called into existence. Through experience and the processing of experience, and thanks to the implicit collaboration between the individual and a given event, objectivity and subjectivity give birth to the field of learning.

I let myself be carried along by my dreams and reverie into the space and time of psychoanalysis, into the analytical field. There I wander through my diurnal and nocturnal fantasies, always ready to continue an adventure which began several – not to say many – years ago.

This book is part of my wanderings. To lose myself in the forest or to pass through the desert of thinking is a labyrinthine experience which has always fascinated me. Jorge Luis Borges taught me that the desert is a gigantic maze. Step by step, as the years go by, I go on learning; that in itself helps me in my journey through life and in my understanding of other people.

Psychotic patients follow their own path through their delusions, often losing themselves on the way. Sometimes they discover or create new spaces in fanciful time; at other moments, they lose track and go round in circles. The delusional ideology is an act of defiance towards the world; its aim is to change the nature of the world and to impose its own rules. But when the psychotic patient's capacities lose their vitality, the delusion 'deflates'. Dis-illusion – the loss of a (delusional) illusion – leads to despair and depression. The patient may then feel the need for support and guidance.

Narcissistic depression (the loss of the delusional ego) brings in its wake a deeply melancholic state which may carry the patient to the brink of suicide. Hospitalization is then the only remedy, and teamwork among carers is vital.

In spite of disagreements between different schools of thought in psychiatry and psychoanalysis, mutual understanding and cooperation are at that point indispensable.

Unfortunately, the psychotic patient often falls victim to disagreements or 'competition' between colleagues. In this way, a dissociative ideology (schizophrenia) will be pathologically reinforced by a social reality which is itself dissociative in nature.

When I work with psychotic patients, I need the collaboration and motivation of the institutional nursing and medical staff.

In 1957, I was attached to a unit in the Sainte-Anne Hospital in Paris, the medical director of which was Dr Daumézon. The Paris Institute of Psychoanalysis invited some members of staff (Dr Daumézon, Ms Aulagnier, Mr Lubtchansky and me) to discuss the relationship between psychosis and institutions.[1] I remember saying that conflicts between different units – or, more generally, between different colleagues – acted in an iatrogenic manner on the schizophrenic's already discordant mentality (the patient's ideas are already in rivalry with one another).

As I set down these thoughts in writing, the problem has not yet been solved. Even though pharmacology has made significant progress in treating anxiety states, in restraining the patient and in treating his or her neurotic and psychotic disorders, the help which it brings is only partial. No pharmacological medication can give the patient understanding. Here too there has to be a good association between the often necessary pharmacological treatment and the attempt to explore more thoroughly the unconscious aspects of the patient's psychotic and non-psychotic thinking.

When I began my career as a psychiatrist and psychoanalyst working with psychotics, there was no 'effective' medication. Some patients still had to be restrained in a straitjacket. I have carried out consultations and treatment sessions with patients physically restrained in this way. It was not easy, but some patients – who were afraid of being unable to control their violence – asked to be maintained in a straitjacket in order to 'preserve' the person to whom they were talking.

From the very beginning of my career, I was confronted with the problem of autism, including autistic spectrum disorder in children, as well as with patients suffering from dissociative personality disorders. I remember the deep-rooted feeling of suffering and solitude I had when I found myself in the presence of these patients unable to convey how they were feeling – in other words, unable to communicate. I learned through time that behind their cold and immobile façade, there was a complex, powerful and violent world.

The psychoanalytic experience, like life itself, is an adventure of love and hate. The psychoanalyst who treats psychotics has to be in contact with his or her own contradictory aspects. In particular, we have to be in touch with our own body, with its sensations, and perhaps even with its psychosomatic reactions when confronted by the patient. Transference and counter-transference form a complex and continuous discourse in which the body-mask (*persona*) and the body-as-experienced by each participant both have a role to play.

For all these reasons, one of my fundamental ideas – it comes up time and again in my writings – is that of the importance of body language in psychotic patients. The body carries traces of the person's history.

Leonardo, one of my psychotic patients, became depressed once he stopped having delusions and hallucinations. In one session, he looked sadly at a crease in his trouser-leg. Alluding to the furrows on his brow, I said: 'Time is marching on. Life has started to move again, and your history is once more taking its course.'

Psychoanalysis allowed Leonardo to express himself not only through his body but also with his clothing. For Paul Schilder (1950), our clothing is part of our body image. Like Flügel, he remarked on the unconscious meaning of the clothes we wear: it is important to note that some people 'live' in their clothing while others give (and perhaps have) the impression that they are dressed up in someone else's attire. The degree of harmony or discord can be seen in the way a person dresses. There is, then, an entire hermeneutics involving the body and its apparel.

Body language is crucial; it precedes and accompanies verbal language. In cases of severe regression, when words fail, it is the body-mask which expresses what the patient wants to say.

That is what I call the archaeology of the body in the transference. Freud was interested in archaeology, in the search for the *arkhaios* in the present appearance of things. The work of the transference is an archaeology of the present. The aim is to discover the memory traces of an unconscious and personal culture through the ongoing development of the transference.

Working one's way through the past rendered present by the transference enables an analytical field to be created. Treating psychotic patients and entering into *their* field also means making contact with their present or repressed emotionality. However, not everyone is able to tolerate and to take on board psychotic anxiety. That anxiety has a material effect on the other participant in the encounter. I have felt it in my counter-transference as a 'concrete' presence, a kind of cloud which swept over me, enveloping me and seeping into me. Sometimes the patient's psychotic anxiety can trigger off inside me an anxiety which is difficult to 'digest' – in other words, my stomach may be keeping me informed of what is going on.

In order to treat psychotic patients, motivation alone is not enough. One's personality must be able to live through the vicissitudes of that kind of psychic and psychosomatic atmosphere.

Tolerating the psychotic transference implies being in contact with one's own regressive aspects and infantile self – hence the importance of the playful transference. It is through this kind of transference, and sometimes through black humour, that we can have access to the delusional experience. I have elsewhere written (Resnik 1973) that direct communication with psychotic patients is not always possible and that some sort of mediation is necessary. In addition, as with every relationship in the psychoanalytic situation, there is always a twofold impact: the patient acts on the analyst, and the analyst on the patient. Certain older conceptions of psychotherapy (or 'moral treatment', as it was called in classical French psychiatry) such as magnetism, suggestion and spontaneous hypnosis, which had some influence on Freud in his younger days, continue to make themselves felt in the regressed states of the transference.

In the 'direct' analysis of psychotic patients, the analyst may often feel caught up in a situation of reciprocal impact which is difficult to manage. That capacity depends on the analyst's personality, degree of 'plasticity', and ability to engage in an adventure which, though enthralling, is often unpredictable.

In this involvement between patient and analyst/therapist (whether the context be individual or group), unconscious events and zones of influence emerge, and they may have a considerable effect on the other participant. Elsewhere, I have introduced the idea of induction (Resnik 1973), which derives from that of magnetism. The principle of induction is linked to the electromagnetic field as discovered by Faraday and Maxwell; Einstein also refers to this notion. When I use the term induction, I am referring to a 'real' or 'physical' phenomenon, an influence which stimulates the other protagonist's capacity for picking up the message which is being sent and unconsciously taking on the role he or she is being asked to play. There is a kind of simultaneous concentration of space and time; what is expressed and 'suggested' by one partner is taken in and dramatized by the other (Resnik 2001 [1973]: 166). Induction, then, is an unconscious phenomenon from body to body which consists in inducing in the other participant a certain kind of positive or negative availability in the service of projection and of manipulation. This situation sets up a transference atmosphere in which the two protagonists 'do things to each other', in other words have an impact on each other. Whether in an individual or group context, one person may try to impose on the others his or her system of ideas – an ideology, as it were, which may or may not be delusional. Thus, the patient may need to make the analyst feel depressed in order to get rid of his or her own depressive anxiety; and vice versa, in a pathological counter-transference, the analyst may try to get rid of persecutory or depressive anxiety by evacuating it into the patient or into the group.

What I have called *indirect communication* refers to a whole series of messages which the patient transmits through various mediators. Through gestures, objects or persons in their immediate circle, patients convey what they themselves find impossible to put into words. Given that the bodily ego of the psychotic patient tends to lose its frontiers and merge with the other person, the patient needs to establish a 'safe distance'. That preventive distance itself may act as a mediator and protect the patient against the tendency to merge with other people: this is what is meant by *transitivismus*. Psychoanalyst and patient thus have to discover the correct distance thanks to which they can 'engage' with each other in the transference without loss of identity.

During the analysis, certain crucial phases of the transference trigger the kind of fundamental transformation which Bion (1970a) called 'catastrophic change'[2] – for example, when the patient, hitherto mentally immobilized and frozen in time, begins to thaw out.

*Glacial Times* is a reference to that critical moment in the life of the chronically ill patient when his or her capacity to feel alive becomes blocked. There is a divorce between surrounding reality and the intrapsychic world. Yet this in itself does not do away with mental pain and persecution. Affects and psychotic anxiety have to be frozen too, in order to avoid intolerable suffering. That is when 'anaesthesia through freezing' begins.

De-freezing implies that we explore the crucial point in time when the patient begins to thaw out and come back to life. This is when mental pain also returns. De-freezing often takes the shape of a psychic haemorrhage or a catastrophic thaw which recalls the biblical story of the Flood. Everyday life has to be negotiated once again. Treading gingerly between suffering and joy, potential mediation makes its way forward.

This book is an attempt to bring together various facets of my work as a psychoanalyst and psychiatrist, working both in the private sector and in institutional settings. My approach is based on the paths I followed in Argentina, France and Italy; it has therefore the character of a transcultural experience. I have chosen to go back to some of my earlier work and show how it fits in with the different stages of my psychoanalytic adventure in the field of psychosis. Looking again at what I have written earlier implies that I have to rethink some of my thoughts as they then were, to complete them and in some cases modify them. The very nature of thinking means that it is dynamic and changing; that is why it is impossible to reproduce exactly what has earlier been evoked. According to Bergson (1939), all evocation is transformation, because past memories are inevitably mingled with present sensations and experience.

Two chapters, 'The Universe of Madness' and 'Glacial Times', were originally written in English. I see them now as contemporary writings in a state of permanent evolution; the updated versions which appear in this book bear witness to the development of my thinking since the time when these texts were first set down on paper – every development in space and time is transformation. Rereading my notes and articles gives me the opportunity of a new dialogue with my own past history, within a time frame which is itself constantly changing.

All through this book, I shall try to communicate how I experience and approach the world of psychosis, through my many years of questioning life itself. My interest in psychoanalysis and in psychosis is linked to the fact that psychotic patients confront us with ontological questions which go to the very heart of our being.

# Acknowledgements . . . with some historical connections

I must first of all express my gratitude to my patients past and present for accompanying me throughout this long and arduous journey. These imaginary travels in the real world have enabled me to explore more thoroughly the language of the unconscious and its implications for life itself. I am grateful, too, to those I have called 'participant observers' – the doctors and nursing staff in hospitals and clinics who collaborated in my research work: Jean Ayme, director of the Henri-Rousselle unit in the Sainte-Anne Hospital, Paris, and his staff; and Professor Ferlini and his staff at the Santa Giuliana Mental Hospital in Verona, Italy.

My thanks also to Professor Pierre Delion, who gave me the idea of reading Rabelais in a different light, especially the *Pantagruel* chapter on 'frozen words'.

My friend, colleague and translator, David Alcorn, has once again succeeded in conveying the sounds and meaning of work done in the Romance languages into English in a way that respects my thinking and the communicative relationship I have with my patients. I am again grateful to him for his sensitivity. One day just a few months ago, as we were working together, he was very moved when a former schizophrenic patient from the therapeutic community I had in Netherne Hospital (in 1958) phoned me from Australia to tell me how she was and asking after my own health. I told David that I had saved that patient from a lobotomy when I was working in that unit; I was able to go on treating her for some years in London thereafter. He was grateful to have witnessed such expressions of gratitude from a patient who now is already a grandmother.

For me it is both an honour and a source of great pleasure to be published once again in the New Library of Psychoanalysis series. England was the place where I was able to develop my understanding of myself and my patients, thanks in the first place to my analysis with H. A. Rosenfeld, towards whom I feel a debt of gratitude to this day. I was fortunate to meet Melanie Klein in 1955 and to attend some of her seminars in the years before she died. I am grateful too to

W. R. Bion, whose seminars also I attended and who was my supervisor in my early work as a psychoanalyst. I later invited Bion to Paris where I organized a seminar with him; it became a public dialogue between us, published in a shortened version on the Internet and, in Italian, in the complete version with many additional notes, where each of our interventions are properly attributed (Resnik 2001a).

Other significant influences on me at that time were the work of E. Bick and Hanna Segal, as well as that of D. W. Winnicott. When I arrived in London, I told Winnicott that he was particularly important for me as a child analyst (one of my first papers discussed his ideas); he modestly told me that the truly important person in London at that time was Melanie Klein.

In this book I recount some of my work with groups. S. H. Foulkes was a landmark figure for me in the 1950s and 1960s; in 1959, he let me use his consulting rooms in order to treat a group of chronic psychotic patients from Netherne Hospital (Coulsdon) who wanted to continue their work with me (I was about to leave for the Cassel Hospital). P. de Mare worked with me as a participant observer – a wonderful friend and colleague. Malcolm Pines, who was close to Foulkes, had suggested that I come to work with him at the Cassel, where he was a consultant. It was at that time too that I met R. D. Laing. He had heard from J. D. Sutherland of the Tavistock Clinic that I had studied phenomenology in Paris under Merleau-Ponty, a subject which interested Laing very much. We would often spend Saturday morning reading and discussing texts on that topic, with a small group of people who shared our interest. He asked me to read, before publication, his book *The Divided Self* (1960), and I asked him in return to read some of my papers which later became my first book, *The Delusional Person* (1973). It was much later that I met J. Berke and enjoyed many a long discussion with him about his work at the Arbours Crisis Centre.

Whenever I return to London – in recent years, I do this more often than I used to – I feel almost as if I were coming back home. The atmosphere in those days was extraordinary and lively, and in spite of some difficulties the 'three groups' within the British Psycho-Analytical Society were able to establish a truly stimulating dialogue; there were representatives of all three groups in the Cassel Hospital, and we would have many lively discussions over lunch.

In my view, Freud's discoveries are an essential tool for understanding our present civilization; the theory of psychoanalysis as well as its applications are indispensable. The Cassel Hospital was important also because the late director, Dr Thomas Main, put into practice there his ideas on therapeutic communities, a name which he invented. I have fond memories too of other medical practitioners with whom I worked there – Drs Pick, Yorke, Alexis Brook, Rubinstein, Kennedy and Templeton. I used to travel by car from Hampstead to the Cassel Hospital with my dear friend Dr Abe Pick; his death at so early an age left all of us – family, friends and colleagues – with a deep sense of loss; a gifted human being, he was already showing great promise as a gifted analyst too. I have always been interested in social anthropology, and was fortunate enough to be able to attend a series of lectures in University College London by my tutor, Mary Douglas, to whom I feel indebted to this day.

In addition to being a Fellow of the Royal Society of Medicine, I am a Guest Member of the British Psycho-Analytical Society (BPAS); although unfortunately I have not been present at the society's meetings, I have been an avid reader of the BPAS Bulletin from its first issue onwards. It was there that I read the stimulating discussions between P. Heimann and E. Glover before they were edited and published in book form by P. King and R. Steiner (1991). Riccardo Steiner is a friend of mine from our days in Italy together, and we still keep very much in touch with each other.

Once again I am both delighted and privileged to be working with Dana Birksted-Breen. Each of us, I feel, has enormous respect for the other's thinking and we have exchanged points of view on many topics and on many occasions. She has been extremely supportive and encouraging all through the preparation of this book, and I trust she knows how grateful I am to her for that also.

Writing is a way of building bridges, of bringing people together. This book is already bringing me closer to England, to my old friends (and newer ones too) in BPAS and elsewhere – all those who are involved in working with the fascinating yet painful world of madness. Madness has helped me to understand that psychotic islets can put on different masks, including religion and politics, and from there disseminate throughout our complex and disturbed contemporary world.

Paris, September 2004

# 1

# Transmission and learning

There is more sagacity in thy body than in thy best wisdom. And who then knoweth why thy body requireth just thy best wisdom?
Nietzsche, *Thus Spake Zarathustra*

The question of the transmission of knowledge and of teaching in general gives me the opportunity to take another look at my own development, to go back to my own training as a psychoanalyst and to return to the subject of my interest in psychosis. Every memory is an emotional and intellectual re-creation. It is a way for each of us to travel through history and go back over the time which is part of the space of our lives.

When I was a medical student learning histology and physiology, I was fascinated by the harmonious complexity of the multiplicity we call the human organism, with its tissue, its texture and its live structure. I was particularly interested in contemplating the 'cosmos' which I could see under the microscope; that magical little window, like a kaleidoscope, would make me dream. As I looked at these 'tissue landscapes', animated by my biological and pictorial fantasies, I felt myself to be both a spectator of and an active participant in a mythological/hermetic event that was both 'surrealist' and fascinating. My curiosity led me to give life and movement to that landscape. A microscopic glimpse of the cosmos thus confronted a macroscopic or global glimpse of my bodily intimacy.

I have always been fascinated by the idea of the imaginary domain which is attached to reality as such. Perhaps the idea of the unconscious was already present, as a kind of unexpected discovery of what had always been there.

Through this phenomenological approach, I am spontaneously sensitive to that imaginary function of the unconscious which opens up whenever light shines on it. The great alchemist, Paracelsus, once said that the faculty of imagination is an inner sun. When I was a little boy, I was fascinated by my mother's black sequinned dress – it gave me the impression of a marvellous

1

universe full of stars. Each of the sequins seemed to me to be a little sun which now I would associate to Van Gogh's *Starry Night* (1889) (Figure 1).

When I look at that painting, I feel myself transported into an imaginary universe full of surprises, one which is alive and at times deeply moving. Through the incandescent trees, we discover a celestial world which is struggling to come alive; each planet seems to be a sun. In this power struggle, Van Gogh's restless thinking traces a cosmic spiral which manages to respect the domain of each of the planets. As an adolescent, Van Gogh was fascinated by birds' nests – indeed, he used to collect them. The Ancient Greeks believed that each star had its own nest somewhere in the heavens.

## The internal world and the philosophy of the unconscious

To return to the inner sky: my discovery of the idea of the internal world in Freud and Klein's writings had to do with the maternal cosmic landscape.

Some years ago, in Europe, I was asked by the publisher Einaudi to write an encyclopaedia article in Italian on the unconscious. Among other works I consulted was Eduard von Hartmann's *Philosophy of the Unconscious* (1931 [1868]), which was published before Freud's discoveries became known. That book gave me a holistic and embodied image of the unconscious. Von Hartmann thus passed on to me the drive-related and lively dimension of an unconscious that was indissociable from the idea of a living organism.

The idea of the unconscious is present in Plato's allegory of the cave. The prisoners, necessary accomplices of their own shadows projected on to the walls, recover their courage thanks to the imaginary dimension present in each of them. They see themselves leaving the cave-body and trying to negotiate with the light of day. The luminous awareness of such a familiar reality has to encounter the unfamiliar aspects of daylight and thereby introduce a dialectic dimension between inside and outside, between night and day. Symbolically, awareness is a lamp which can shed light on the multifarious and enigmatic inside-ness of every human being.

With reference to the idea of multiplicity, in *Group Psychology and the Analysis of the Ego*, Freud (1921) makes use of Gustave Le Bon's notion of the 'collective mind' as an expression of a group's unconscious phenomena. The individual who is part of the group is quite different from that same individual seen in isolation. This can be understood as two different categories of the same human and social phenomenon. Freud uses the idea of regression in groups, in which members lose their individuality and, carried along by their drives, identify with an uncontrollable and instinctively acting crowd. Freud was describing the inner person and his or her relationship with groups, which brings to mind certain of Plotinus' ideas. In Alexandria, Plotinus speculated on the relationship between mind and body in the inner man: that relationship, he argued, was not to be

Figure 1 © Photo SCALA, Florence. Vincent van Gogh, *The Starry Night* (1889). New York, Museum of Modern Art (MOMA) © 2004.

thought of merely in terms of reciprocal influence, but rather as a kind of 'primary mixture'. Plotinus wrote of original chaos, of the primitive relationship between body and soul, of the consequences of the mixture of soul and body, and of the fact that the soul uses the body as a tool. That metaphor, drawn from alchemy, was to reappear during the Italian Renaissance, in the court of Urbin, under the guise of Marsile Ficin. In his study of the cosmos, the pattern of the celestial bodies in the sky constituted the visible signs of God's will. Astrology and hermetism played a major role in neo-Platonic philosophy; Ficin translated from Greek to Latin the *Corpus Hermeticum* attributed to Hermès Trismegistus, considered to be one of the wisest men of ancient times.

For von Hartmann, the idea of *corpus* was linked to that of the unconscious. I had the imaginative impression, as I read his work, of a holistic and embodied unconscious: the unconscious with a mask. That enabled me to conceive of a complex and abstract idea of the unconscious, within the concrete image of a living anatomical and physiological multiplicity.

During my early years of psychoanalytic training, when I first came into contact with Freud's concept of the unconscious, I often wondered about the link between mind and body, about the unconscious in the life of the body and

3

its destiny in life. My travels through life have prompted me to confront the notion of time both in normal states and in psychopathology. I was thus able to see life as a biography which has its roots in the dawn of individual history but which may be 'uprooted' in psychosis. At the beginning of my career, I already had the idea that psychosis was a mental alienation from bodily experience, a migratory flight from reality, from mental space: a metempsychotic fantasy.

As regards the phenomenology of psychosis and the semiology of the encounter (movement and time in the body, transference and counter-transference), the image which I find particularly striking is that of patients who suffer from melancholia. Their almost immobile masks epitomize the extent to which time has slowed down for them: almost to a standstill. The sad, slow delusion of the melancholic patient stands in stark contrast to the acceleration of time and the excitability which are typical features of manic states. Whether in the cyclic phenomena of manic-depressive states (diachronic dissociation) or in the temporal discordance of dissociative personality disorders (synchronic dissociation), the main element common to both is the lack of harmony – and sometimes outright disharmony – among the component parts of the mind. The inner world is undoubtedly a living community which is often in conflict, one in which the 'inhabitants' live through the vicissitudes of their existence.

In schizophrenia, that kind of temporal disharmony is expressed as ideas which are isolated from one another (psychotic islets) or as patterns in conflict which resemble the cosmic universe we see in Van Gogh's *Starry Night*. In that painting, we can observe the sudden intrusion of turbulent thoughts between the planets, thoughts which try to impose themselves brutally and with delusional omnipotence.

A delusion, say ideologists such as Destutt de Tracy, can be seen as a system of ideas.[1] The word delusion (in German, *Wahn*) designates an idea or set of ideas which is more or less organized (*Wahnideen*). Etymologically, the Latin word *delirare* means 'to deviate from the furrow', to deviate from the norm, from the straight and narrow, from the ideology sown by a given culture. In English, the term is 'delusion', which derives from the Latin *deludere*. This notion seems to me to be crucial if we are to have a proper understanding of what a delusion is; in my conception of the psychoses, these different words are significant. In the Latin *de-ludere*, there are two fundamental ideas: in one, delusional thinking is 'off-side', because it does not follow the rules of the game; in the other, there is the idea of dis-illusion. Throughout this book, the reader will observe that a delusional ideology is based on an illusion which defies the reality principle: a utopian illusion, because the therapeutic process entails a dis-illusion for the psychotic ego ideal and ideal ego. I call this phenomenon deflating the delusion. The deflated delusional object then generates a profoundly melancholic state: narcissistic depression.

The fact that an idea is delusional does not imply that it is illogical. Its logic, nonetheless, may be quite different from what we normally mean by logic: it is the logic of delusion. Freud (1911) explored delusional thinking in some depth in his report on Senatspräsident Schreber, who experienced in his own body the transformations which were taking place in his world. Schreber felt that he was someone else, a woman, because of an omnipotent insemination generated in the erotic transference with respect to his psychiatrist, Professor Flechsig. After several acute psychotic breakdowns, Schreber became chronically ill; thereupon, his delusional passion cooled down somewhat, only to be brought to life again in his *Memoirs*. I mention Schreber in this context in order to emphasize the importance of body language (and the dialogue with celestial bodies and rays) and of the implications which it entails in psychoanalytic practice, especially with psychotic patients.

The science which involves decrypting bodily masks is called physiognomy (Lavater 1775–1778). In my first book (Resnik 1973), I wrote not only about the body image in psychosis but also about the physiognomic reality of the body. To describe someone in terms of his or her appearance – the mask or *persona* – implies that, as Antonin Artaud put it, 'the mask is linked to the person as the shadow is to the body' (*The Theatre and its Double*, 1938). People express themselves through the masks they wear, their general attitude and their position with respect to the world around them. In a psychotic crisis, the individual risks losing that self-image. Through their habitual masks, psychotics identify with the characters in their delusion and lose their sense of personal identity.

According to Freud (1923), the psychical ego expresses itself through the bodily ego, in other words through its mask. Among psychoanalysts, Winnicott studied how the concept of the body evolved in childhood and adulthood from a developmental perspective linked to the ideas of corporization and personalization.

### My clinical experience with psychotics and psychosis

Thinking of the patient's 'psychopathological physiognomy' takes me back to my very first experience of treating psychotic patients in groups; I was in Buenos Aires at the time. That first encounter with a group of chronic psychotics took place in 1952, in the local psychiatric hospital. I remember the impact that event had on me: the existence of verbal language was something quite exceptional. The dominant factor was silence. The group's 'face', its mask–*persona*, was inscrutable, silent and tense. From time to time, the expression changed and, with a grimace which was both moving and distressing, indicated pain. At other times, it seemed to be more open, fluid and approachable, but with eyes which were penetrating and intrusive.

In this work with long-stay psychotic patients in a group context, I had at the time the impression that, in a poignant universal landscape, the life of the unconscious seemed at times to be immobilized inside a puzzled institutional or group body. The dominant feature – macroscopic in the group and microscopic in depth – was the impression of a *pathos* which was blocked and imprisoned inside a mummified body. That appearance was expressed somatically as a disturbingly apathetic mask.

The individual or group unconscious is a bodily reality: a body which shows itself (*phainestai*: 'that which appears'), like an organism which reveals itself and lays itself open to the watchful eyes of others.

The unconscious speaks through its mask (the body) and reveals itself to the skilled interpreter in a form of language which is essentially drive related and actualized. The instinctual drives are thus seen to be a natural force. They express themselves, telling of their history and its affective vicissitudes by means of the body in a language which is simultaneously ancient and modern.

I attach considerable importance to phenomenology and psychiatric semiology. Psychoanalysis is a hermeneutics the object of which is to unveil – with due care – the intimacy of one's being. Given the private and secret aspect of every therapeutic encounter, there has to be an ethical dimension in the transference. The psychoanalyst who 'contemplates' the other person in an individual or group context is at the same time being 'contemplated'. The transference is an experience which is based on the emotional reciprocity of two worlds: that of the patient (or group-patient) and that of the psychoanalyst. The transference is also part of a movement, of a *translation* in space and time. Since each of the moving parts belongs to a given cultural system, a confrontation between different cultures is inevitable. In that sense, every transference phenomenon has a transcultural dimension.

Since I am myself of foreign extraction, this aspect is of special interest to me.

A transcultural approach is required, an attitude which both respects and seeks out different climates and personal or transpersonal value systems. In an article I wrote called 'Psychose et institution' (Resnik 1988), I discuss the complex set of problems associated with representations of mental illness and delusions in different societies. I quote Emile Durkheim's (1895) definition of society as a social organism. Though his conception is pragmatic and in part mechanical and positivist, his perception of the phenomenon is intuitively correct. For Durkheim, society is not a system of organs and functions but a living whole. Some years later, von Uexkull (1920) provided a dynamic glimpse of the relationship between the *Innenwelt* and the *Umwelt* in all human beings.

The notion of living organism contains the potentiality of a cellular society, and vice versa – the body of every human being and of every living entity, with all its functions and value systems, is characteristic of any given culture. The relationship between man and environment raises the problem of otherness and of liberty.

According to Hegel, being conscious of one's corporeal boundaries is already a way of overcoming, to some extent at least, the fear implied by being in and with the world. Every experience of an encounter is basically dynamic. It is part of a system of reciprocal *translations* and transformations which becomes manifest through the transference relationship. As a living organism, the human being is a biological reality (the life sciences) and possesses a bi-logical system (Matte-Blanco 1975) which belongs to the dialectic relationship between conscious and unconscious. In his discussion of Freud's writings, Ignacio Matte-Blanco (1975) put forward the hypothesis of two logical systems in the human mind. The one is expressed through our ordinary logical thoughts: it divides, separates and differentiates by means of asymmetrical relationships (typical of consciousness). The other conceives of, experiences and feels reality to be homogenous and symmetrical (typical of the unconscious). All of this is part of a complex multidimensional network: the coexistence of different dimensions in the same place at the same time (Bria and de Risio 1992).

The unconscious, therefore, could be thought of as a group multiplicity which obeys specific social and cultural principles and which invites us to develop more and more keenly our research into inter- and intrapsychic diversity.

With reference to the multiplicity of the unconscious, Bion argued in his lectures at the Tavistock Clinic (Bion 1961) and in his seminar in the United States (Bion 1978) that the answer (to the unconscious) lies in the group. He was replying to a question on the sense and meaning of reality; is the question of the existence of a fundamental reality a valid one? In the seminar, Bion was asked whether he thought that a group can have an unconscious. He replied: 'I wouldn't want to abandon that idea; nor would I want it to obscure the discovery of what else the group has' (Bion 1978: 23). Later he would link what he said there to the idea of a *basic language* in a group context.

Bion and Lacan are in agreement over the idea that the unconscious is like a primitive and universal form of language which is simultaneously contemporary.

## Psychotic thinking and language

My own experience has helped me to understand that between patient and analyst, 'from unconscious to unconscious', there is confrontation. In the same vein, at the origin of the transference there lies an encounter between 'trans-actional languages'. Every analytic experience, individual or group, requires a creative (or re-creative) search for a common language. This common language has to be created or invented on the basis of the linguistic inheritance of each of the protagonists.

The unconscious-as-language is expressed not only through thoughts and words but also by gestures and by the whole physiognomic and physiological expressiveness of the life of the body. Every movement of the body, every conscious or unconscious event, is linked, as von Hartmann (1868) pointed out, to the present dynamic reality of a living organism.

7

There exists a proto-language made up of a more or less coherent and more or less integrated set of sensations and meanings; this may sometimes take on the proto-structural character of a prelinguistic or linguistic grouping.

In her exploration of the early stages of thought processes, Melanie Klein paid particularly attention to the senses; she was therefore especially sensitive to anything which concerned proto-language and proto-mental phenomena. She took from Freud the idea of the image (in Jung, the *imago*), though she preferred to talk of unconscious representations, of fantasies and, above all, of internal objects. Her idea of the internal object means that it is not simply the equivalent of an image (in the sense of two-dimensional reality); it is above all a three-dimensional object reality which has depth, just like the body itself has. In such a case, the unconscious and pre-conscious space (in which language at the symbolic level appears) participates in a reality which is multiple, complex, dynamic and alive. In this mental space, the internal objects are transformed into *dramatis personae*. Like actors, they dramatize the fantasies which correspond to each human being's unconscious and private life. It is also in that space, whether the person be awake or asleep, that the infantile ego experiences its playful adventurousness. In *The Interpretation of Dreams*, Freud (1900) compares the dramatization of the dream to the playing of a child.

Oneiric dramatization is also a re-creative group experience in which actors and audience mingle with one another or confront one another, depending on the oneiric role they are given by the 'stage manager': the dreamer him- or herself. In *Le Groupe et le sujet du groupe*, René Kaës (1993) shows how the group can be characterized if we adopt the hypothesis of a living unconscious. The question for this author is the idea of the group as such: 'The paradigmatic form and structure of an organization of intersubjective links, seen from the angle of the relationship between several subjects of the unconscious, generate specific forms of mental structures and processes' (Kaës 1993: 12).

With reference to what I have been developing in this chapter, I would perhaps add to this the impact of soma-psychic processes on the individual and collective organism.

In the late 1930s, Kurt Goldstein made a considerable impact on the French tradition with his book on the structure of the organism (Goldstein 1939). He wrote of the organism as a complex cell-like and metabolic community which is fundamentally harmonious. In pathological situations, he added, the social behaviour of the organism breaks down, loses its morphological and physio-logical logic (its structure), and disintegrates into a state of disorder which is potentially catastrophic. He suggested therefore that, from a biological point of view, the behaviour of an organism can be either appropriate or inappropriate. Goldstein (1939) emphasized the idea of the organism as holistic, as did von Hartmann (1868); the life-giving processes do not become exhausted in one isolated response. Under normal circumstances, all parts of an organism partici-pate in different ways in that holistic nature.

This idea is similar to that of the *Gestalt*. Gestaltism, or psychology of form, was developed by Paul Schilder (1950), a pupil of Goldstein's, and further refined by Wertheimer, Kohler and Koffka. The *Gestalt* can be thought of as a set of patterns or shapes in a state of change or transformation in the environment.

## The idea of field

Kurt Lewin (1963 [1951]) also developed the idea of *Gestalt* in terms of a set of *Gestalten* – forces and shapes of structural expressions in a recreational or playful context. He began his series of experiments by observing schoolchildren during their break, in order to study the psychological influence of the environment. He tried to discover connections between the forces involved in the children's play and those which belonged to their educational environment. The result of that exchange of forces (conflict between forces or patterns of forces) was expressed dynamically and structurally by demarcating a field. Lewin introduced the idea of a force-field. He demonstrated the tension between them, in other words the forces in play at any given moment and at any given point in the field. He used the notion of positive and negative valency (induction upon or by an object), which Bion was later to borrow. Lewin wrote also about the concept of the social field within which the child has to deal with a great number of demands and issues that have their origin in the social and physical aspects of the environment. Another interesting notion is that of the direct or indirect influence exerted on one another by the objects which make up the field. From 1926 on, Kurt Lewin wrote several major papers on the social dynamics of sets and their atmosphere; these have played a decisive role in the development of the concept of the field and group dynamics.

The concept of the field amplifies that of the transference in psychoanalysis. The experience of the transference also unfolds within a given field and at a specific time; these are the constituent elements of what in psychoanalysis we call the *setting*.

## Transference in groups

With reference to the idea of plurality or multiplicity in the transference field, and with the notion of the psychoanalytic process as a backdrop, I would now like to describe and to try to communicate something of what transpires in a session with a patient in individual treatment.

Maurice is 45 years old and at time of writing has been in analysis with me for more than ten years. At the beginning of the analysis, he was quite inhibited and unbending. It was very difficult for him to break free of the defensive armour which protected him, especially against his own drive-related impulses and against an environment which he experienced as threatening. After many years of psychoanalytic work, his ability to express himself, his freedom and his playful ego – which had been asleep, as though anaesthetized – woke up and enabled him to reveal an abundance of emotional and intellectual qualities which he could henceforth put to some use.

In one session, he was expressing, in great detail, his childhood feelings and fantasies linked to the atmosphere of the session itself. After a long pause, he added: 'This silence is noisy.' That strange way of putting things became a reality thanks to his free associations. He went on: 'I have the feeling that I am hearing noises; I can hear my mother breathing.' (I think that he was referring also, in the transference, to my breathing.) He then continued:

> That reminds me of my nightmares as a child. I knew that my mother was sleeping with my father in the bedroom next door; sometimes I felt she was coming close to me with her breathing, and that would frighten me. I wanted to be with her, but at the same time she terrified me. Sometimes it was not my mother's breathing, but that of some stranger or other, a ghost standing by my bed. I was terrified, I tried to hold my breath in order to paralyse time – and paralyse the ghost too.

In another session, Maurice could feel the silence and the darkness of my consulting room.

> I feel that I'm in danger here, like in the middle of a forest. I feel myself to be at risk in this forest full of wild animals ready to attack me . . . They are not real animals, but shadows of animals which are watching me, observing me, hiding behind the trees. Sometimes it's the shadow of a threatening tiger or lion. All that reminds me of when I was a child and had those old nightmares in which I was at the mercy of terrifying presences. I can see myself in my bed, hiding under the blankets, whispering 'Mummy' and hoping she would come to me. At that point, I would try to hold my breath and not swallow my saliva. In the end, during one of these nightmares, my mother answered my whisper and came to see me. All the noises and all the ghosts disappeared as if by magic, then my mother too disappeared, because she went back to bed. I know that all those ghosts came from inside my head. Nowadays I would think of my *inner night*, of everything I did not know about myself, everything which, thanks to my analysis, is now becoming clearer and has a more well-defined shape. But I'm still afraid that there could be a mad presence inside me which might waken up and overwhelm me.

Then Maurice added: 'But I know that this is all fantasy and that they're not real monsters. I'm not afraid of them any more.'

In another session, he dreamt that he had to sit the Baccalaureate exam in the classics. 'There are exam papers in Greek, Latin and Philosophy. I feel well prepared.' On another occasion, he dreamt that he was to sit a physics examination in Dutch:

> I don't speak Dutch, and I know nothing about physics; I'm more interested in psychology. I know that having psychoanalysis means making contact with a world that speaks a language with which I am not familiar.

I had the impression that this was a reference to the language of the unconscious. He associated the physics exam to his own physical state, and in particular to the tenseness of his muscles and his inflexibility – a condition he had suffered from for many years, the main symptom of which was a severe backache.

He was thereafter able to relax and to feel himself less 'uptight' in his body, in his physical reality. He associated the dream of sitting an examination in Greek to classical mythology, which he enjoyed especially since he was beginning to understand his *personal myths*.

For me, interpreting Maurice's dreams meant learning about the mythology of his private language which was to a considerable extent foreign to both of us – 'double Dutch', in a way. The Latin examination was connected to his success in studying and in translating into a 'Latin' language (that of his analysis with me) what was unknown and hidden in his internal forest, in the darkness of his unconscious. He associated the philosophy examination to his ability to think, in other words to establish links between his ideas and make connections to what he had learned in his work with me. He was henceforth able to associate creatively – and to be a creative associate in our work together.

His ego, present in the session, was able to re-create his childhood nightmares without being as terrified of them as he had been before. He could not recall having played very much as a child, but with me he was beginning to play and to put himself 'in play' – in other words, to take the risk of communicating and dialoguing.

The transference and counter-transference are part of an exchange, a dialogue, mutual communication. The word transference – *Ubertragung*, in German – implies the idea of crossing from one place to another. (*Uber* means 'on', and in *trag* there is the implication of passing through, of something which is transferable.) There is also, for me, the highly familiar image of the *traghetto* in Venice – crossing from one side of the canal to the other in a gondola. We could say that, in psychoanalysis, there is a continual *traghettare*, a twofold movement from one side of the canal to the other – from patient to psychoanalyst and vice versa: a double transference.

The word *Ubertrag* includes the idea of transmission, of translation (from the Latin *translatio*) and of negotiation. The transference is thus a highly complex notion; the idea of translation and transmission enables us to have a dynamic and holistic image of the psychoanalytic process.[2]

In the transference, transmission is of two kinds: the sharing of a system of communication (reciprocal transmission) which initiates the transference in the psychoanalytic process (individual or group). It is playful transmission in particular (when it becomes manifest or is aroused) which characterizes the 'good' development of the psychoanalytic process. This is another way of saying that, in psychoanalysis, true transmission is a shared situation (the participants play, they play with each other, they put themselves 'in play' and take risks). This is more of a horizontal and relation-based act (synchronic) than a vertical or solemn one (diachronic), in which a 'subject-presumed-to-know' delegates some of his or her power to a child, to a junior.

In addition, there is a playful internal *traghettare*, if the infantile ego is aroused (the infantile transference). This takes place between the conscious and the unconscious aspects of each protagonist, or between the patient-ego and the psychoanalyst-ego. It may be expressed in the psychoanalyst or, in a more specular fashion, in the patient (the patient-'speculum' reflects the other person's image in a perhaps idiosyncratic way). The locus of this (re)search constitutes the field in which we work and communicate in the transference; it becomes a workshop in the true sense of the word, as well as a training school – the two-way transmission is shared by both partners.

When Maurice became less blocked off, he was able to make contact with the world of his instinctual drives (the wild animals), with the wealth of feeling which his senses brought to him and, above all, with his unconscious fantasies. From time to time he would become depressed, a state which was expressed as lethargy. Lately, just after the death of his father, his lethargic or somatic depression was more marked. For a long time, he was unable to talk about his father sufficiently. The shadow of the absent object, to paraphrase Freud (1917 [1915]: 249), that of the father, appeared in his dreams and fantasies in the shape of a threatening presence, in which Maurice recognized one of the ghosts of his childhood nightmares. Over time, the father's shadow turned into a tolerable and even warm-hearted presence. Maurice's body became less lethargic and apathetic. His mental space was more available for integrating the loss of his paternal object, whom he loved in an ambivalent way. He was then able to discover, in the newly awakened Oedipal myth suffused with sensations and fantasies, the non-persecutory (and even somewhat amicably inclined) aspects of his father. That helped him to understand the mother–father–child triad (the family) and to come to terms with the world, his world.

To talk of internal objects is a way of conceiving of the inner world as a mental space which contains a multifarious reality, one which is dominated by the 'noises' of the primal scene and infantile anxiety. At times, during a session, the old nightmares – and sometimes dreams linked to the primal scene – are shrouded in mist or hidden by clouds, thereby highlighting an atmosphere which is full of 'fantasy apparitions'.

As regards clouds, I would like to describe some aspects of another of my patients: Gustave.

He was lying on the couch, with me seated behind him, and we felt sub-merged by an oppressive atmosphere. In my counter-transference, I felt as though a threatening cloud was spreading over me and Gustave. That impression became even stronger as a pause occurred in what the patient was saying, a pause which enveloped and paralysed me. I said to Gustave: 'What an oppressive silence!' 'Yes, it is oppressive,' replied Gustave, lethargically. I too fell half-asleep, locked in a shared drowsiness that I tried unsuccessfully to shake off. The cloudy silence kept on growing, with apparently nothing to stop it. Fortunately, a few minutes before the session was due to end, Gustave began to associate, saying in a murmur which was both depressed and depressing:

> I see myself in my new home, trying to frame the paintings I had stored in the attic. I can feel the general disorder of my house growing and growing. I felt it was important for me to work on framing those pictures.

It was at that moment that, with Gustave's help, I began to understand the therapeutic function of the patient. He was the one who was dealing with the pollution of the transference climate. He was suggesting that I needed to discover or to create a framework or setting for the melancholic cloud which was over-whelming us and contaminating us. From the denseness of his silence, replete with worrying sensations and experiences, there was also at least the potential for a constructive solution which would put a frame around the anxiety that, emanating from his body, was transmitted to my own, and vice versa.

Putting a frame or setting around the session meant that we could give some shape (*Gestalt*) to an uneasiness that was difficult to circumscribe, and thus make it available for the transference. At any rate, we had to establish a framework for exchanging, for *traghettare*, for transmitting and transferring fantasies which came from both sides of the 'canal'. The framework was needed so that a setting could be established such that we would have a shared 'play area' and thereby process the work of the analysis in the requisite field.

After we had worked through that silent yet active impasse, the atmosphere became less oppressive, less polluted and more breathable. In a letter to Reneri written in 1638, Descartes (1954) said that in order to think, one must be able to breathe. An overwhelming and oppressive political climate does away with freedom of thought. That is what Descartes meant by 'I breathe, therefore I am.'

It should not be forgotten that the infant's first relationship is not with the mother's breast, but with the surrounding air or, rather, with the mother-ether (compare Fenichel's (1953: 221–240) idea of respiratory introjection). Going from intra-uterine to extra-uterine life requires a *negotiation* with air. Breathing or not breathing goes to the very core of primitive fantasies or proto-verbal nightmares which are part of every individual's prehistory or proto-history.

Birth implies a difficult *formative* relationship, just as with any important life event at the beginning – and this is the case too when one begins psychoanalysis.

13

According to Melanie Klein (1952), the problem of the transference and of the transmission of the way in which one experiences a relationship begins with life itself. To my mind, that primitive object relation, first with air, then with the mother's body (and implicitly with the father), is not particularly clear nor well defined at the beginning of life. For me, it is rather vague and nebulous, as indeed I felt it to be in that regressive session with Gustave and in several sessions with Maurice.

In describing the infant's early states of mind, Frances Tustin (1986) uses the expressions 'sensation shapes' and 'sensation objects', which is one way of saying that our earliest representations are cloudy and have no well-defined frame.

The idea of the frame which gives formative shape to something brings to mind other examples of the multiplicity of the external and internal worlds and other experiences which were difficult to frame and thus to understand.

One day, between two sessions, I went for a walk along a narrow medieval street near to my consulting rooms, the rue Visconti in Paris. I was looking in the windows of the little art galleries. I stopped at a shop which sold African art, then at a theatre bookshop called Petrushka (which reminded me of my Russian ancestors), and finally near the workshop of a picture framer. I then thought of the paintings of an artist friend of mine, Carmelo Ardenquin, whom I much appreciate and whose characteristic way of working is to design the frame for any given piece of work in terms of the content of the painting itself: form and content are thus part of an indivisible reality. That very day I had to write an Introduction to an exhibition catalogue of his paintings.

While I was walking back to my consulting rooms, I was thinking of the group of patients who were waiting for me (I was by then a couple of minutes late). Several patients were already inside and were looking at the paintings on the walls of the room in which we worked. Someone said: 'We've just been talking about frames.' I replied: 'How interesting! As I was walking along the street, I was thinking about that too.' As we sat down, one of the participants said: 'It's true that we were looking at the paintings, but I think too that we were worried about your not being here. You know we need you to create a frame and shape the setting of the sessions.'

The frame or setting of a group is not necessarily an Alberti window (the Renaissance model of a window), it is an informal frame which has been cut out in an apparently shapeless way, with no precise form – but which gradually comes to have a specific shape; it takes shape, in other words, it has body.

That episode is associated in my mind with another which also had a profound impact on me. In this other group, one of the participants was a young 23-year-old woman called Marie, who had been hospitalized several times after a series of major psychotic breakdowns. One day, during the session, she had a severe dissociative crisis. Nobody was able to contain her, not even the two psychiatrists participating in the group. The only patient who managed to restrain that catastrophic experience was, in his professional life, a picture framer. That session was for me a living metaphor of the notion of the psychoanalytic setting in a group situation; it is of value, too, for individual cases as well as for some institutional contexts.

## The group as a multiplicity in motion

A group of neurotic or psychotic children or adults brings even more obviously to mind the idea of a holistic organism. It is for me a multifarious reality, complex and kaleidoscopic, always in motion, always alive. However, in psycho-pathological states or at certain crucial stages in the life of a group, that moving plurality may freeze, become static and lose its vitality. This corresponds to stressful situations or to psychotic experiences present in the group dynamics.

The structure of all groups is fundamentally schizoid. We often use a metaphor such as 'the group thinks that . . .' or 'does not think that . . .' (in cases of mental paralysis, such as in groups of psychotic patients). The group is a reality, but a plural one, because it is made up of individuals whose personal histories are different, even though they may share some common points – what Ezriel (1950) called the common denominator. Every person who speaks in a group does so implicitly in the group setting as such, in the group body as it were. Every group, on a formal level, is integrated by each of its members, and at each new encounter the members have to 'regroup': rediscover the group space within its own particular membrane (a word derived from the Latin *mem-brum* – limb or member) and temporality, in other words its 'remembrance'.

Time and memory constitute history-as-it-happens, a history which takes shape within its own structural dynamics. Every body (or body image), every living assembly which comes together as a group, is transformed by that very act, in other words it reassembles then comes apart. In his development of the idea of body schema, Paul Schilder (1950) describes how a group comes together then breaks apart. The group is not an accumulation of separate individuals nor is it always a global entity – it is both of these, in other words it undergoes continual change and transformation within a living history.

In the famous Wednesday meetings which Freud held in his rooms – within his 'membrane', as it were, in his home – he was preoccupied by the diffi-culty he had in trying to control the regressed states of his group of pupils who were being 'formed'. Certain participants, swept along by their transference (even before Freud had fully explored the notion), felt a compelling need to relate their infantile sexual experiences and, more generally, their anxieties. I have the impression that Freud, overtaken by events and overwhelmed by his own counter-transference, needed to ask his colleagues to help him establish a proper framework or setting for that situation. I have also the fantasy that those events made it materially obvious that psychoanalysis had to be given a sound institutional basis – in other words, that the twin aspects of learning how a psychoanalyst works and training in the practice of that profession had to be properly organized.

## Transmission and learning a profession: the craft of the patient, the craft of the analyst

In this chapter, I am attempting to convey a living image of my thoughts on my own training and training in general. Being a psychoanalyst means experiencing the vicissitudes of a long process of learning where the kind of 'transfer' is not the same as *mission* or as *trans-mission*, whether it be mystical and religious (conversion) or political (the search for power). In training, what I try to transmit to those who are seeking to learn is the true essence of our craft. When I use the term *craft*, I mean not only that of the psychoanalyst but also that of the patient: the craft of the patient.

If psychoanalysis exists, is it because of its therapeutic function? One of the questions which Bion often asked of himself – and of me too, as it happens – was: 'If Freud had been a painter, would he have invented psychoanalysis?' There is no easy answer to that question. Psychoanalysis is a methodology, a technique, a hermeneutics – but above all a craft (the craft of the psychoanalyst) and an art. As a medical practitioner, Freud was concerned with pain – by his own pain, and by the anxieties that pain may cause. His initial research work had to do with cocaine, which he himself used in an attempt to alleviate his mental and physical suffering.

It is not by mere chance that I have linked Bion's question on Freud-as-painter to what I have been saying about paintings and picture framing. Not long ago, I took part in an interdisciplinary colloquium at the Cini Foundation in Venice on the theme 'Landscape: from Perception to Representation'. Contemplating one's internal world – what Freud's concept of the observing ego designates by the term *insight* – can be seen as a representation of a private landscape, one that is often hidden by the clouds of the unconscious.

In my view, Melanie Klein's conception of the internal world is an experience of multiplicity and grouping as far as the internal objects – mobile or immobile, often in conflict – are concerned. The overall frame of such an internal landscape also acquires a bodily dimension: mental space is the entity which, externally, is called the experiential body (Husserl's *Leib*). For me the anatomical body image (*Körper*), individual or group, possesses internal and external membranes (the group is continually re-forming/regrouping and coming apart).

Paul Federn (1953) describes the frontiers of the ego in terms of a peripheral sensory organ. He explored the relationship between the ego as a dynamic entity and its frontiers as a manifestation of its integration; it is this relationship which is upset in states of depersonalization.

In *The Ego and the Id*, Freud (1923: 25) writes: 'A person's own body, and above all its surface is a place from which both external and internal perceptions may spring.' He argues that 'the ego is first and foremost a bodily ego [*Körperlich Ich*]; it is not merely a surface entity, but is itself the projection of a surface' (1923: 26). 'It may thus be regarded as a mental projection of the surface of the body [*Psychischer Ich*].' This means that, under normal circumstances, there is no dissociation between the mental ego and the bodily one but a spatial correspondence, one which has two aspects: that of the body image and that of the image we have of our mind. In states of depersonalization or split personality, the mental ego and the bodily one are split apart or, better, dissociated: a state of non-correspondence. In derealization, there is a projection of one part of this dissociated state which, by reason of that projection, becomes externally split-off: projective identification with an everyday landscape.

I have just mentioned painting as an analogy, and what now comes to my mind is a musical memory. I was a young man when, one day, I was fortunate enough to be present at the recording of some chamber music, written for eleven instruments by Alban Berg, under the direction of René Leibovitz. I could not then have imagined that, several years later, I would get to know him personally and become one of his friends. I was by then already passionately interested in Freud's writings, and as I listened to Alban Berg I felt that the language of the unconscious bore a very close resemblance to atonal or dodecaphonic music. At any rate, that music moved me deeply and undoubtedly made the instrumental chords of my mind vibrate. My father was a musician, so I was always very much influenced by the world of music. Thinking of the mind as a musical instrument is an idea which came quite spontaneously to me, in a more or less tuneful and gentle way.

After several years of personal analysis and many years of study, I am convinced that our mind is fragile, delicate and highly sensitive to music. The mental ego and the lived-in body are living instruments, instruments of research, of therapy and of life itself. These instruments are so sensitive that they have to be frequently retuned. Hence the importance of further analysis, in several portions as it were, for every analyst who is aware of his or her limitations. Each has to choose an appropriate tuner, whether it be in individual or in group analysis. I am convinced that a phase of group analysis can be rewarding, but only if the 'tuner' has considerable experience and proper training.

Individual psychoanalysis is complementary to psychoanalytic psychotherapy in a group setting. It is a way of apprehending the same landscape from different perspectives, and that experience cannot but be rewarding for the observing ego in each of us. In addition, in every group there is a social reality and the presence of public opinion, sometimes oppressive but nonetheless necessary (like the chorus in Greek tragedy, as I shall explain later in this book).

With some patients, I have found it helpful to recommend this twofold approach. They are two different types of experience, which over time prove to be complementary. I do feel, however, that if these two approaches are undertaken simultaneously and with the same analyst, this can give rise to some difficulty.

Problems of training, transmission and learning are interconnected. One can transmit only what one has learned. The very word 'transmission' can be problematic in itself. We do not transmit what we have learned in the same way that an order is transmitted in the Army, the Church, a political party or a charismatic sect. Transmitting one's analytical experience – individual, group or institutional – requires *sharing*; it is a 'serious' kind of playing, in the infantile transference. The transference is a two-way transmission of learning: one learns from and with the other person.

Learning a craft like psychoanalysis takes place within a given context (a matrix) by means of a complex form of transmission. In order to be able to understand the patient, whether the context be a dyad or a group, one has first oneself to learn the craft of being a patient. A psychoanalyst who has been a 'good patient' will be able to understand the other person *from patient to patient*, while managing to keep in mind the vicissitudes and responsibilities of his or her professional role (in the counter-transference). This is true of individual psychoanalysis as well as of group analysis. There must be a period of training in an analytical group if the psychoanalyst is to understand patients-as-a-group (or the group-as-patient).

All training in psychoanalysis has to be rigorous. Creating a training group or bringing together several such groups in a harmonious way in order to maximize their potential requires that differences be put to one side or at least tolerated: the ideological narcissism of each group has to be acknowledged in order to reach some form of global consensus. The creation or consolidation of any training institution requires that an appropriate institutional organization be established in as flexible a way as possible without losing the necessary 'frame'. It needs a maternal body, a matrix, which is able to contain as much multiplicity and contradiction as possible. So much diversity in a totality (mother) requires a paternal function to structure it adequately. In other words, the concept of mother-and-father-as-a-couple has to be integrated, as well as the primitive imago of the combined parents, particularly in moments of regression.

## Conclusion

My intention in this chapter has been to make more explicit the paths I have followed in my own training and the vicissitudes thanks to which I have been able to approach the world of the psychotic child or adult. Making contact with the primitive experiences of every analysand, psychotic or not, in some ways resembles a 'journey to the centre of the Earth'. From another perspective, we could say that it is a matter of entering into the primal cave of humankind's geological unconscious which lives inside each of us. In that sense, it is quite appropriate to speak of the Earth's geological destiny, embodied as human nature. Freud described psychoanalytic research as an archaeological dig into the unconscious. From an onto-phylogenetic perspective, he made a link between chronic psychosis (where the ego is frozen) and the kind of utter destitution which prevailed in the Ice Age.

Freud's paper *A Phylogenetic Fantasy: Overview of the Transference Neuroses* was found among Michael Balint's papers; it appears to have been given to him by his friend and mentor, Sandor Ferenczi.[3] It could well be described as an archaeological discovery in the history of psychoanalysis. Freud therein refers to what Kraepelin had to say about *dementia praecox* being a state of 'real' self-castration. The term 'real' is an allusion to the reality, in the psychoses, of the abandonment of all love-objects, the decrease in sublimation of all sorts, and the return to auto-eroticism. In his view, hallucinatory episodes are an attempt to cure that disorder.

We could argue also that, faced with a feeling of death (total castration) and regression to an ice age (in the case of 'frozen' chronic psychotic patients), the ability to generate delusions and hallucinations is one way of thawing out and experiencing the reality of psychosis. An acute psychotic crisis or paranoid state, in a petrified and chronic psychotic patient, may actually be an experience of coming alive.

Infant observation is a recommended part of psychoanalytic training in the United Kingdom; why not devise a complementary group experience in order to complete one's training as an analyst? That is my way of looking at the problem of training as a whole: I am convinced that in order to be a good group psychoanalyst, one has already to have proper training as a psychoanalyst.

Nobody can teach – in other words, transmit – what he or she has not learned; at the same time, we all go on learning – our training could go on for ever. The exercise of individual and group psychoanalysis is in itself *ongoing training*, thanks to which we can continue learning our difficult twofold craft of being both patient and psychoanalyst.

# 2

# Bodily identification in psychosis

In the vast collapse of our civilization, among the ruins of Europe, our thoughts, as they are wont to do, roam somewhere in the past. Anxiously, through the obscure labyrinth which here and there is pierced by the sun's arrows, they seek out – in an eternal return – shapes which resemble those that surround it and offer it the key to the mystery of present time.

Romain Rolland, *Empedocles of Agrigente*

Whenever we ask ourselves 'Who am I?', 'What am I made of?', 'What do I look like?' the idea of similarity or of a primary identificatory model emerges at the same time. Similarity evokes the notion of dissimilarity, a certain idea of otherness. The psychoanalytic experience is an investigation into time within the space of the transference – an archaeology of the present, as I said in my Preface.

When we ask ourselves 'Where am I?', 'Where do I live?', 'Where is the place I call my home?' is this language in Heidegger's sense of the term? Or is it not rather the body-as-language? The identity of the *locus* of one's sentient being is thus affirmed as co-extensive with the body, where the self discovers or rediscovers its 'sameness' (Voltaire). To exist means to be somewhere: *Dasein*, as Heidegger put it. In this way, every human being has a *locus* in the space and time of history.

Time leaves its mark on the expression of the body-mask, on its *persona* – human beings communicate with their environment through the wrinkles on their brow, their attitudes, their gestures and their oral manifestations (vocal gestures). The individual constructs his or her life through an emotional coexistence. It is via relationships that life takes on its historical configuration, its history emerging topographically through the mask. The mask (*persona*) is related to the personality, just as the shadow is to the body. I have developed this idea in my book *The Delusional Person* (Resnik 1973). The word person – *persona*

– derives from the Etruscan *phersu*, literally a mask worn in the theatre, whence personality. *Phersu* corresponds to the Greek *prosopon*, which gave the word *prosopeïon*, mask. The person as actor of his or her own history presupposes the idea of movement – hence, of a living body – and the inevitability of cultural transformation. It is this which makes for an ongoing dialogue between human beings and their environment, between the space and the time of their history.

These thoughts, derived from my experience as a practising psychoanalyst, have led me to formulate a certain number of hypotheses as to the nature and identity of the body. Winnicott used the word *corporization* to describe the awareness of the fact that one has a body which is one's own and in which one lives; this is a constituent part of the process of personalization (see Chapter 1 of *The Delusional Person*, Resnik 1973). I would like the present chapter to be a meeting-place for the location and meaning of the speaking body, a *locus* in which these various perspectives can confront one another. The idea of location itself evokes that of a *locus*, of the geography of bodily experience and of one's ideological position in the presence of another person. What matters in psychoanalysis, as in life, is the experience of an encounter (Hegel's *Erfahrung*, Dilthey's *Erlebnis*), that is, an experiential event.

## To be or not to be

I shall begin by saying a few words about Caroline, a young psychotic woman who suffers from a very severe schizophrenic condition. She has been in analysis with me for several years now.

In one session, Caroline, lying on the couch, stared at her shoes for quite some time, then said: 'I feel like I've been knocked off my feet'. She associated to her feeling of being 'not with it', somewhere else, depersonalized.

That was Caroline's way of raising such questions as 'Who am I?' and 'Where am I?' It was also her way of trying to help the analyst: 'If you think I'm really in the place you see me, you're mistaken. As a matter of fact, I'm somewhere else.'

Caroline may not have been 'in' her Self, but the 'somewhere else' was not too far off – a condensed way of expressing ambiguity. She may have been 'knocked off her feet', but concretely, in the session, the 'somewhere else' was just beside me, the analyst sitting behind her on a chair. At any rate, I was at that point her nearest neighbour, and therefore the person whom she could cathect the most.

After a brief silence, the patient reported a dream: 'A young woman is scratching my husband's back – I feel very unhappy as I watch them.' At that time in her life, Caroline wanted a divorce; in her dream, another young woman has already replaced her by her husband's side. Caroline associated also to the

21

analytical couple (patient and analyst in the transference). I understood her to mean that she felt very lonely and that she was 'somewhere else', not 'in' her body. Sometimes, indeed, she felt that she did not have a body at all and that she was transparent, a pure 'spirit'.

This phenomenon corresponds to what I have described in 'Cotard's Syndrome' (Resnik 1973). Here, Caroline was not only dissociated from her own self but also 'divorced' from her shadow. She was part of an ill-assorted couple made up of her body and her shadow. When she has no body or feels 'knocked off her feet', she needs to burrow her way inside someone else. In the dream, she saw a depersonalized image of herself, a double who was trying, by scratching, to burrow her way into her husband's body.

Since their separation, Caroline unconsciously felt abandoned and unable to live inside her own body, hence her need to force her way into someone else. In the dream, that other person was her husband, but in the transference I was the 'someone else'. Like young children or small animals, she tries to burrow her way into a safe place and live inside someone else's 'house'. Pathological projective identification consists in abandoning one's own house-body and in living as a parasite within someone else. But in losing her own *locus*, Caroline lost her very identity.

The dream occurred just before a holiday break – in other words, just before a 'separation', a temporary divorce between Caroline and me, one which was difficult to tolerate at that particular stage in her analysis. She needed to find safety somewhere, a welcoming maternal body during the time a man/father-figure was abandoning her.

Psychosis implies alienation from one's own body. Whenever the experience of one's body becomes too painful, psychosis can unconsciously 'decide' either to dissociate the self emotionally (anaesthesia and shutting-down) or to move the self elsewhere. This 'elsewhere' may be either outside the body or some internal organ. When mentalization is too painful or too persecutory, the ego has to evacuate all suffering into the body or part of the body: this is the hypochondriacal solution.

As to thinking processes, sad or persecuted thoughts may decide to emigrate, to move house, to relocate. The myth of the transmigration of souls corresponds to the fantasy of being reborn in another time, another place, another form: this is what we call metempsychosis.

Projecting oneself inside someone else's body (or into another naturally occurring form) is manifested through a kind of 'physical transvestism' (dressing in someone else's clothing, imitating that person's gestures). Projecting oneself inside someone else's mental space is manifested through 'mental transvestism' (imitating the other person's thinking, feeling oneself to be that other person). In the former situation, the self tries, by projective identification, to acquire the other person's bodily shape and character, where that person is loved and admired. In the latter situation, the self imitates the other person's way of thinking – his or her ideology, in other words. We encounter this kind of phenomenon in our professional work with colleagues – some analysts (and some patients) believe they think like Freud, Lacan or Klein. Such people have no personal identity in this domain; they identify with their ego ideal, represented by some idol or group or sect.

I use the word 'transvestism' in the sense of 'false identity' – Winnicott's 'false self', in other words. The self is searching for its identity in some other person rather than within its own body, its own personality, its own *persona*-mask. In 'transvestism', the individual is dressed up physically or psychologically in a foreign identity. Idealization of the charismatic ego is similar to metempsychosis in so far as there is a common basis in the myth of being reborn, which is a utopian aspect of projective identification. In literature and in philosophy, metempsychosis plays a major role in Plato's *Symposium*. For Plato, the *anima* feels as though the body is a tomb or a prison: our body is *soma*, our sepulchre *sema*. The words *soma* (body) and *sema* (sign) reflect the ideology of the Hellenistic civilization of the time: we are born into a body, we live in one and we die when our body dies.

When the body becomes a prison, the self develops feelings of claustrophobic anxiety. If we feel overwhelmed, we break free of our material being in order to force our way into someone else's body or mind. According to Paula Heimann (1942), projective identification is a way of forcing the object to make room for the self. In such circumstances, there is only a pseudo-identification. This is a very interesting concept, because it can help us to be more precise about the limits which govern normal and pathological projective identification. If the projection is too violent, it becomes intrusive – the other person is desecrated or profaned, as it were.

With its 'grandiose' idealization, imitative identification conceals deep feelings of envy. If we are to understand properly Melanie Klein's concept of envy, we must not forget that it is based initially on admiration. However, true admiration, manifested as genuine appreciation of and gratitude towards the object, must be distinguished from envious admiration, which is destructive. Allied to envy, there is a kind of admiration and ingratitude which leads to hatred and violence. For Ferenczi (1909), introjective identification generates a sense of identity; projective identification always implies a pseudo-identity.

Personally speaking, I prefer to call projective identification 'stereoscopic identification'. Here what is important is the three-dimensional view – it is not a flat projection on to the surface of the object, but one which requires depth, one which goes *into* the object or *engulfs* the object, to use Bion's term. In 'Further Remarks on the Neuro-Psychoses of Defence', Freud (1896) defines projection with reference to a stereoscopic view of the world:

> I was able to hope that I might trace the compulsion of paranoia, too, to repression. The only peculiarity was that the thoughts which arose from the

23

unconscious were for the most part heard inwardly or hallucinated by the patient, in the same way as her voices.

(Freud 1896: 178)

I understand Freud's use of the term *Verdrängung* to mean 'repression of the suppression'. The patient, Frau P., had felt she was being criticized by internal voices until, one day, a significant change took place: she no longer heard any voices coming from inside her – the voices of her neighbours took over, and they too began to criticize her in no uncertain terms.

It seems to me that, for Freud, repression (*Verdrängung*) and suppression (*Unterdrückung*) imply that certain psychological phenomena can move around in the external world inside other people, as though they were being carried by these objects. This mechanism is what he calls projection.

> In paranoia, the self-reproach is repressed in a manner which may be described as *projection*. It is repressed by erecting the defensive system of *distrust of other people*. In this way the subject withdraws his acknowledgement of the self-reproach; and, as if to make up for this, he is deprived of a protection against the self-reproaches which return in his delusional ideas.
>
> (Freud 1896: 184)

I would therefore argue that the idea of 'stereoscopic projection' or 'projective identification' (Klein) is already present in embryonic form in this early paper of Freud's.

The psychotic experience corresponds to the mechanism and ontological feeling which involve projecting oneself, leaping across the gap in search of a place of freedom: a place to which one can escape and begin life over again, in another nest. That is how the fantasy of metempsychosis is expressed in the psychotic universe.

The word 'psychosis' comes from the Greek *psyche*, meaning 'spirit, breath of life', and *osis*, 'animation'. It therefore means animating, setting life in motion. I find it pleasant to refer to the mythical metaphor of the transmigration of souls in order to define psychosis and pathological projective identification (which is, as I have said, a 'pseudo–identification'). It involves a flight towards some other *locus*, another body, another life.

When psychotic patients can no longer put up with their own life-space (body, skin, clothes and so on), it becomes impossible to keep their feet on the ground, as Caroline told us. The psychotic person will therefore try to fly upwards and off via a kind of 'migrating levitation' in order to find some way of alleviating the pain – a new existence, a new haven, a new outlet, a new port, a new portal. 'Port' and 'portal' both come from *poros*, meaning 'passageway, gateway'. A portal or doorway lies at the threshold between what is secret (sacred) and what is public (profane). Knowledge also requires a passage, a transgression

24

of the threshold. It is for this reason that there are rites of passage – the ritualization of an ethics of knowledge, of recognition, of rebirth.

'Keeping one's feet on the ground' implies the capacity to maintain contact with one's own individual reality as well as with that of other people – with the world, in other words. According to Caroline, however, 'being down to earth is sheer hell'. That is why the psychotic has to escape, to get away from the earth and from the terror which is part of it; the patient has recourse to his or her ability to levitate mentally and fly upwards into the cosmos (the ascending current). The body feels lighter and can begin to 'float'. That ascending current – levitation – represents the idealized aspect of the delusion. Beginning one's ascent towards the cosmos is a way of escaping from everything which belongs to the terrestrial world and of setting out on the quest for a celestial body. Sometimes thoughts or feelings do not levitate continuously; they wander about with no apparent aim in mind. Perhaps mental dis-order, down-to-earth, is seeking a universal cosmic order. Finding a home or a maternal container is not enough in itself; there has to be someone or something to help reorganize the disorder: the paternal figure who provides the spinal cord and vertebrae which are necessary elements in every structure. This phallic function is complementary to the maternal one. Alongside the persecutory image of the combined parents as described by Klein, there is a parallel desire to construct a positive image of parents who, with their 'good' combination, can offer the child a harmonious model.

Caroline saw her body vanishing, going up in smoke. When she felt anxious, she felt more alive – so much so, indeed, that she could not bear it: at that point, she would have the impression that there was just emptiness, a void, where her body should have been.

> Whenever I feel agitated and nervous, I have the impression that there's a big hole where my body ought to be, an abyss which I have to fill up, so then I smoke, one cigarette after the other.

The smoke filled Caroline's body, which gradually faded away, evaporated, went up in smoke. But sometimes the smoke went beyond the frontiers of Caroline's body and invaded the surrounding space. The transference atmosphere would then become hazy and blurred.

A great hole where the body should have been and the abyss which Caroline spoke of – which she had to fill up with smoke – correspond to an experience of lightness and emptiness of a body which has lost its soul. This is reminiscent of Plato's *Gorgias*, with its image of the cask which is leaking and unsound – an empty body/cask with a hole. The image of the leaking barrel was no doubt inspired by Pythagoras.

Caroline then began to feel afraid of the dark. When she was in bed, she felt that there was a strange and frightening presence somewhere in the adjoining room. Sometimes she saw a spirit wandering through the darkness – that terrified her. She associated the wandering spirit to her father, who committed suicide just as she was beginning her analysis.

The 'decorporized' presence of her father's spirit on the other side of the wall – a disquieting proximity – echoed her own feelings of gloom and lifelessness; she too felt dead. Caroline said of her father that he was always 'full of life'. For her, he had been a sign of vitality, someone who had helped her find her bearings as she wandered through life. The ghostly presence of her father was a kind of condensation of his simultaneously lively and persecutory spirit. This image of her father represented also a lively but troubled aspect of Caroline herself.

Reintrojecting her living ego (projected on to her father) into her leaking body full of holes was often confused with an intrusion on the part of her troubled and panic-stricken self. According to Enrique Pichon-Rivière (1947), psychotic patients feel that madness comes from outside the self; they do not, therefore, realize that reintrojection is what is actually taking place. The father who had committed suicide took on an alienating or unbalancing aspect which was merged with a mutilated fragment of Caroline's own ego during the cata-strophic experience of her acute psychotic crisis. These ego fragments evacuated into the world (*Verwerft*) are dead entities which drift along like wandering ghosts.

The work of mourning accomplished in the transference enabled Caroline to transform her nightmare – the ghosts – into a dream which was bearable and intelligible.

Freud's paper on mourning (1917 [1915]), together with that of Klein (1940) and Griesinger's (1882) concept of 'basic depression', underlines the importance of mourning processes in the genesis of mental illness. Freud sees in melancholia the expression of a deep depression which more often than not is linked to psychosis; this is close to certain aspects of the idea of 'basic depression'.

For Caroline, the ghostly shadow of the absent object which came back to her became intelligible once it could be related to the shadow of her own ego, merged with her paternal object. I have elsewhere said that loss of the object is above all loss of the relationship which the individual had with that object. Part of the ego always accompanies the object in its absence. Freud writes of the shadow of the object falling on the ego (1917 [1915]: 249); I would add to that the fact that the shadow of the subject (the person suffering the loss) which accompanies it must also be reintrojected if the mourning process is to be properly worked through.

In my *Mental Space* (Resnik 1990), I describe another patient, Monsieur Tavel, who was able to mourn his mother's death only after he had dreamt that he was going to fetch her buried body and bring it back home. In that way, the shadow of his own exhumed ego was finally able to thaw out, thus enabling him to shed tears.

## An iron body

The second patient I want to discuss is Henry, who was 21 years of age when he began his analysis with me. He was accompanied by his mother for this first visit. During puberty, he had had an acute psychotic (schizophrenic) breakdown. As his interlocutor/analyst, I witnessed some surprising mythical and delusional metamorphoses in his universe.

I came to realize that the split between his real (waking) world and his delusions had to do with the fact that this was the only means he could then find to express the tremendous pain and distress he felt. In one session, Henry reported a dream in which various buildings made of clouds and smoke were all tangled up. He could recognize a Greek temple with its columns and statues: 'It makes me think of some of Magritte's paintings,' he said. I had the feeling that, at that point, Henry was unable to differentiate between dreaming and daydreaming, between oneiric reality and ordinary physical reality. In his delusion, his daydream, he was trying to construct or to reinvent a world of his own made up of clouds and smoke. This construction gives us some idea of the infinite transubstantiation of the psychotic patient's pain and distress.

Henry's ego was in complete confusion as to the frontier which separated these two spaces and qualities of reality; his divided self, lost among the clouds and the smoke, had no sense of its own identity nor of that of the world. Who was he really? What was the nature of the world which surrounded him? Where was he? Where was he to locate the environment in which he lived – and which lived inside him? Was it in his experience of a dream-delusion or of a delusional dream?

In the course of his analysis, Henry, with my help, thought deeply about the content and the texture of his dreams. We tried to differentiate them from his delusional reality. With clouds and smoke – his eyes open or closed – he could always reinvent a new universe, albeit a short-lived one, one that would vanish into thin air. It may have been for that reason that Henry often said of himself that he did not really exist; he seemed always to be about to fall apart. Indeed his delusion began with the feeling that he was dispersing and dissolving into the universe as a whole.

The initial theme of his delusion had to do with feelings of being sucked up into the cosmos. When he was out of doors, he felt he was in danger of being engulfed by some superior power. That was why he wanted to 'feel his weight' – he hallucinated a kind of heavy armour-plating made of iron, so that the sheer weight of it would always keep his feet on the ground. In this way, he could resist any form of antigravitational pull. The iron was also an echo of his coldness and 'hard as steel' aspect. When he was in pain, Henry had to 'freeze' and cover his thoughts and feelings in a metal jacket.

Before all this, Henry was quite 'of this world', with his feet firmly on the ground. He used to be a strong outgoing young man, as solid as steel and as hard as nails. As though he were a gladiator in Roman times, he had equipped himself with solid armour-plating in order to protect himself against any blows he might receive and to preserve his integrity. We called this period of his life 'the Iron Age'.

From solid armour-plated protection – which at the same time is a kind of prison – to constructions made of clouds and smoke, there is quite a 'substantial' semantic transformation, one which points upwards. There is a kind of ascending movement of matter in which each phase represents a certain stage of development and an identificatory mode. Each state of matter corresponds to a particular 'state of mind', a particular way of feeling and being. Our first perceptions are sensory in nature (Susan Isaacs (1952) adds that our first fantasies are sense-based/sensory experiences). These first feelings have to do with hot/cold, hard/soft, full/empty – the idea of the 'hole'. These are the experiences of matter which can 'support' sensations ('sub-stance' means what is standing underneath to provide support). In her studies of autistic children, Frances Tustin (1986) showed how the most primitive feelings and sensations seem to the child to have no shape – they are shapeless. As a reaction to this, and given their difficulty in conceiving 'form', autistic children need a hard object (as opposed to a soft and fragile one) which has a definite shape in space, so as to create their own autistic objects. The nature of matter is in itself a 'shape' – a way of experiencing and of thinking about reality; this experience, however, has to be given 'context' or be contained in order for it to acquire first proto-symbolic and then symbolic (metaphoric) status. In autistic children, this contextual frame is of an extreme kind.

At one point, Henry went through a megalomanic phase in which he had a kind of dream – a vision, perhaps – in which he discovered in the sky a sort of giant spermatozoid which looked like a comet. He commented:

> That makes me think of my father and my birth; and of my mother's womb – and my grandmother's too. Also, I'm thinking of the Virgin Mary and the birth of Christ . . . I think my dream/vision is a kind of cosmogony. I see myself as a sort of god invested with tremendous power.

I asked him: 'What kind of power? Sexual? Cosmic? Perhaps with eyes which are capable of a sidereal ejaculation?'
Henry replied:

> But now that I feel much more 'alive', I'm afraid of that world. I'm afraid of falling into the clouds or into the sky – and I'm afraid of falling to earth and crashing to the ground.

He was trying to escape from the earth, which terrified him – but at the same time he was afraid that the cosmos might engulf him. Perhaps he could ejaculate himself, catapult himself towards another planet and begin life all over again – a divine, grandiose existence. Henry then had to cope with his pathological ideal ego and omnipotent magical powers. As his megalomanic delusion began to subside, he felt disappointed, 'deflated', furious with himself. He became very depressed and on several occasions tried to commit suicide.

I define that kind of condition as 'narcissistic depression'. Here we do not have the loss of an object as such, but rather – and above all – the loss of some part of the self or of the ego: the ideal, megalomanic part, the pathological ego ideal. Losing his delusion implied for Henry losing all his sidereal power and falling to earth like a deflated balloon. That disillusion was expressed in the transference as attacks on me, the analyst, who had made him face up to the reality of his delusion.

In the transference, there was often the wish to annihilate the analyst – and especially to reduce my 'power' to nothing. This was Henry's way of nullifying differences and distances, of engulfing the other person within the cloudy atmosphere of his psychotic universe; he hoped thereby to defend his pathological egocentricity and protect himself against narcissistic wounds. Psychoanalysis had brought his delusional myth back down to earth. Usually, when psychotic patients lose their delusions, that means for us professional carers that their mental health is improving; the patients themselves, however, may feel very weakened, wounded narcissistically and betrayed.

The narcissistic wound which opens up at that point is a kind of intolerable 'mental haemorrhage'. In Henry's case, the bleeding could be stopped only once I had helped him discover another image of himself, one which related to his non-psychotic part. For a time, when Henry felt himself to be omnipotent (in fact he had no vitality at all, he was cold and mechanical), he thought that he could perhaps 'raise his spirits up' all by himself, like a crane on a building site. His subsequent fall weighed all the more heavily on him; depersonalized psychotic 'de-pression' is a heavy load to carry.

Henry would often go back to his mechanical being because it helped him not to feel pain. He would say: 'I'm like a pet animal, I do whatever my mother wants just like a little dog.' He could feel this kind of dependence in the transference situation with me. Sometimes he would act the monkey and imitate me – a robotic monkey which moved in a mechanical way and was completely without feeling. He would say also: 'At times, I feel I'm a powerful electric machine which needs only one man to control and drive it.' He again referred to the image of a crane: 'A crane can lift loads which weigh a tremendous amount.' That was Henry's way of letting me know how heavy his depressive burden was.

In his psychotic experience, Henry's heavy body lost all of its vitality and was transformed either into a robot or into a small mechanical animal; at other times – this depended on his state of mind – he was an all-powerful machine. How and why did this metamorphosis take place? Henry's infantile ego, hidden in the depths of his being but still alive somewhere, resurfaced and came back to life in a world full of mechanical animals and soft toys – the playthings he had when he was a boy. It often happens that toys find their way into the shadows, dead areas and reified parts of the patient's infantile ego. For Klein, the inability to play (in children who are emotionally very inhibited) is an important sign of illness. In one of her articles, 'The Importance of Symbol-Formation', Klein (1930) has interesting developments to make on this topic, thanks in particular to her analysis of a severely psychotic boy with obvious autistic traits.

Sometimes Henry felt nostalgic for his Iron Age. Once he said to me:

> I feel blunt and hard as if I were made of iron – Cartesian, dogmatic, categorical. I always need to see where my thinking is leading and not have my head in the clouds, in some vacuum or other . . . May I take off my raincoat?

For some time past he had constantly worn a raincoat and only rarely took it off.

> When I feel hard, there's something which is opposed to experiencing and listening; I feel empty, with no thoughts and no feelings – in fact I'm dead. I'm strong and hard like steel, but I'm dead. I have the impression that my head is in the grip of a steel vice the jaws of which are tightening all the time . . . And I have burning sensations in my stomach too.

I pointed out to Henry that his stomach was therefore a place where life was continuing, it was alive (though painfully so) – digesting such a heavy burden as his must indeed be difficult.

> In the street [he answered] people get on my nerves. I feel ugly and weird and afraid. Now I can see myself dead, like in the dream I had yesterday: I could see myself alive on a cinema screen, but at the same time I was in the audience and I was dead . . . Sometimes I feel weak and empty . . . I've always needed to wear a raincoat these past few months. I feel lazy . . . Nothing can be done about it, I've lost all hope . . . I'd like to overcome my weaknesses, I'd like to control myself and everybody else around me. Sometimes I can't feel my body any more – and sometimes I can't even see myself, as though I'd become invisible . . . On the other hand, there are times when I'm too visible and everybody looks at me.

Between visibility and invisibility, permeability and impermeability, transparency and opacity, the hyperreality of his delusion ploughed its dogmatic furrows in the real world. The delusional ego of this young patient dressed up as an erudite alchemist and rivalled with the analyst in a defiant challenge. Henry often said he felt old, and he liked to evoke the image of an elderly or ancient alchemist pouring over his phials; his delusional ego opposed psychoanalytic knowledge with its own learning, its own transformational ideology. Henry preferred that kind of learning, which attempted to transform the very substance of matter (in a delusional way, of course), rather than accept the idea of coming back into a world of ordinary standards.

## A petrified body

I would like to illustrate the argument of this chapter with another clinical case. Peter was a 40-year-old architect who had been in psychoanalytic treatment with me for many years.

When he first consulted, Peter was finding it more and more difficult to 'move on' in his life and make contact with other people. Emotions could not get through the frontiers of his body, and this gave him an inflexible and inhibited appearance. He was distressed by the fact that his thinking was also beginning to lose any flexibility it may once have had. In spite of the fact that he was remarkably clever, his petrified and petrifying attitude gradually prevented him from working, being creative and living his life. There was often a contrast between his inflexible and tense 'mask' on the one hand, and a bright look in his eyes and a pleasant smile on his lips on the other. Peter was playing a part, he was imprisoned inside some stage character or other. Who, then, was the real Peter?

For many a long year he guided me, in the transference, on long journeys through time and space. In his wanderings in the biblical desert, he introduced me to Moses leading the people of Israel, and to Isaac, almost sacrificed by his father Abraham to obey God's injunction. Peter was a well-educated person, and he tried to win me over with his charm and his marvellous narratives in an attempt to draw my fascinated infantile ego to him; I would then be following him in his wanderings, just as the Hebrews followed Moses.

Peter said: 'The first temples which were built in the desert by Moses were made out of canvas; on those tents, they often drew an image of the Sphinx.' The Sphinx, symbol of knowledge, painted on the canvas of the tents or graven in stone (Peter/*petrus*), here represented an omnipotent and dogmatic erudition which often became paralysing and petrifying. Like the Sphinx – always reluctant to reveal its secrets, it conversed only with those initiated into its cult – Peter spoke in a series of metaphoric and enigmatic narratives.

He had lost his father while he was still a boy, and for some time thereafter he was separated from his mother. During the Second World War, he was detained in a Japanese camp for children (at that time, he and his family lived in Indonesia). His memories of that period of his life are apocalyptic. He had experienced the separation from his mother as being ripped apart, broken and cut up into thousands of pieces.

31

In his delusion, Peter often identified with Socrates. He imagined himself lecturing to thousands of people in the Parthenon. Sometimes he was Moses, or Abraham the father of Isaac. He imagined he was 'inside the skin' of charismatic paternal figures who were capable of bringing together thousands of people in one place. These 'thousands of people' to whom he would lecture made me think of his fragmented childhood when he felt he had been cut up into thousands of pieces. I made that interpretation to him. He responded quite emotionally – for his petrified being, experiencing pain and making contact with it were still difficult. His hypersensitive infantile ego was kept hidden, 'walled up' inside his *persona*-mask. His delusional identifications made him want to play the role of a therapist/shaman who would be able to repair his ego broken up into thousands of fragments.

One day as he arrived for his session, he seemed very upset. He had just come from a trip to the Louvre, where he was a regular visitor. That day, he had 'encountered' a young Pharaoh – a bas-relief of Akhenaton. Something in the Pharaoh's eyes had caught Peter's attention and he had spent a long time staring at the sculpture. He had been especially intrigued by the look of pain on the young Pharaoh's face (Resnik 1984) and the way his neck seemed to twist – again painfully – backwards: what was Akhenaton looking at? In which direction did he really want to go? What was he regretting? 'I had the impression that the statue was about to start moving, that the young Pharaoh was going to keep moving forward, after this interruption in his progression'.

Peter had just had a significant experience which was almost unhoped for. Like an eternal adolescent, immobilized at a particular moment in life in statuary reality, Peter-Akhenaton had experienced a painful vibration in his body, fixed in stone and in time. The twisting of the neck expressed an attempt to break free of petrification and millenary immobility. The feeling of pain heralded the return to life, the return of feelings and sensations inside his body. Peter could at last perceive in himself a 'turning point'. He had spent so much time looking backwards, going back in time – but now he was about to begin moving forward again and to catch up on lost time.

Peter-Akhenaton had spent so much time imprisoned in stone – prisoner of an omnipotent and petrified present which annihilated both past and future. The absence of any future implied quite literally that he had nothing to look forward to. The 'travels' Peter had undertaken 'thousands of years ago' were only leaps around the space and time of his own past history. After a long period of life with no fluidity to it, Peter's encounter with Akhenaton, frozen in a painful grimace, offered him a mirror image of his own life paralysed in time.

For Peter, that encounter proved decisive. Petrified time suddenly began to move again; Peter was back in contact with life – and also with death, as a life-experience. 'My true nature is pathetic,' he said. 'I'd like to move forward, but I'm afraid. I know I have to grow up and leave adolescence behind me, catch up on all the time I've lost'.

32

In the sessions that followed, the image of Akhenaton grew and grew and became disproportionately inflated, monumental, transcendent. Peter was not yet able to tolerate the feelings which were becoming alive inside him. With his tendency towards morbid rationalization (Minkowski 1927), Peter gathered as much information as he could on the young Pharaoh's life. According to Minkowski, morbid rationalization is part of the thought processes of schizophrenics, who are deprived of the capacity for emotionally assimilating anything which concerns movement and time; they tend to transform their feelings into a mechanical kind of logic. Here, Peter discovered that Akhenaton too, like Peter himself, had rebelled against his father. With some emotion, he told me how, as a young boy, he liked to compete against his father in all sorts of games – he would try to see which of the two could run faster, jump higher, etc.

In a certain sense, this play was repeated in his relationship with me, through the mirror of the paternal transference. Peter would challenge me; a symmetrical/mirror interplay would then ensue, with the idea of who held the more 'power' again coming to the fore.

From time to time, Peter-Akhenaton would try to break free of his statuary character, leave this frozen time and put an end to the permanent state of war (a cold war) between him and the father-analyst. Sometimes too he would feel nostalgia for a warm relationship with a paternal figure. At times like these, he would try to get in touch with his playful infantile ego. Some degree of ambivalence surfaced: he would hesitate between keeping up a defiant attitude on the one hand, and, on the other, wanting to reintroject a new paternal image, a benevolent one this time. Through his infantile ego (i.e. in the infantile transference), the patient was looking for a non-persecutory father, a structuring guide who would help him reintegrate his true identity, his substance, his living 'matter'. The word 'matter', from the Latin *materia*, means 'maternal substance' and implies the idea of something underlying and supportive. This support makes for a fundamental structuring skeleton which integrates the qualities of the maternal function as well as those of its paternal counterpart. In order to construct a protective suit which will prove effective, the link between these two sets of qualities must be a good one. In other words, there must be a positive 'combination' of the feminine and masculine parts of the ego, so that tasks and attributes may be adequately shared out and harmonized.

As the analysis continued, the delusional megalomanic image of Peter-Akhenaton became less inflated. (It is interesting to note here that the word 'folly' comes from the Latin *follis*, meaning bellows or wineskin.) His feelings of omniscience and omnipotence abandoned him; Peter was in great distress, he felt disheartened, very 'down'. The narcissistic deflation of the ego corresponds to the feeling of dis-illusion or to loss of the 'power' of the narcissistic ideal ego, which can no longer recognize itself in the ego ideal's mirror. As I have earlier pointed out, I call 'narcissistic depression' the feeling of loss which involves not the object but the ideal ego, pathologically idealized, as is the case in delusional psychosis (Resnik 1980).

Peter continued his research into the Pharaoh's life. In one session, he spoke with a great deal of admiration in his voice of the Pyramids of Egypt: 'Basically, since I'm an architect, I'm a direct descendant of the great pyramid-builders. The pyramids date from even earlier than Akhenaton, and they're immortal.' Peter was thus searching for a new line of descent, just as Akhenaton had done in his day. Peter saw himself as the son of the great architect Senemuth – to some extent, then, as a descendant of that great demiurge and creator. This again had to do with an exaggerated inflation of time, a monumental time, fixed for ever in stone and defying eternity. Peter again became immobile, put on his 'stone clothing' and went back to his dogmatic learning. He talked again about Moses, Abraham, Isaac – about the 'sacrificed child'. In the transference, the roles were distributed. When Peter played father-Abraham, he would be inflexible in his dealings with his son, in spite of the latter's pleas: the analyst-Isaac was to be led to the slaughter. When Peter became Isaac again, he was to be sacrificed by his father-analyst.

Peter liked to feel he was my father – this allowed him to teach me things. When he was in the role of the son – or of the patient – he felt wounded narcissistically. When he managed to project on to me the figure of the boy Isaac, I had to allow myself to be 'circumcized' of my position as analyst and learn everything I knew from him, the mentor. In fact, he made me a present of a very interesting book, *Isaac and Oedipus* (Wellisch 1954). Reading that book proved very helpful. The first chapter is entitled 'Infanticide': this helped me to realize that one of Peter's complaints had to do with his father's death. His father had died during the war and Peter had been left to fend for himself, cut off from his mother, in the concentration camp for children. Consciously, he loved and admired his father enormously, but unconsciously he had never forgiven him for having abandoned the young boy he then was. For children, mourning is a very difficult process, because in their representations and value systems, parents are just not supposed to die. This is an important point which must be taken into account if we are to understand mourning processes not only in children but also in the child who lives within every one of us (Resnik 1971).

Over time, Peter began to feel more alive and less of a statue. He could feel pleasant sensations of warmth – which from time to time changed into a painful sensation of being burned. His body was less inflexible and less cold because time was henceforth marching on. His internal warmth enabled him to break free of his fossilized posture and to look backwards as well as inside himself.

A restructuring Oedipal situation was being set up – it replaced his earlier destructive and persecutory Oedipus complex. He became more aware of his selfish ego, the arrogance he had carried with him for a thousand years. Awareness implies tolerating narcissistic wounds and accepting that one's delusional value system has to be called into question. It implies also facing up to the pain and suffering which always accompanies 'sudden' growth (compare Akhenaton). Money-Kyrle (1978: 417) put it thus: 'the patient, whether clinically ill or not, suffers from unconscious misconceptions and delusions'.

## A frozen body

Mr V was a tall, slim, young man, somewhat ceremonial in his manner. From the first time we met, he gave me the impression of someone who was extremely inflexible and cold. Something mechanical emanated from his body.

He was carrying a large package, and near the beginning of the session he handed it to me. I could not refuse it, because it was suddenly thrust upon me. It was a very heavy object. Mr V said: 'This is a gift for you. Please take it and open it very carefully'. 'Can I open it now?' I asked. 'Yes, but be careful, because I have wrapped it up in a very special way in order to protect the gift.'

'Why,' I said. 'Is it fragile?' I began to open it. It was a big book which bore the title *The Dolomites: 360 Degrees*; it contained magnificent photographs of the Dolomite mountains, which lie to the north of Venice. I looked at them with him; they were desolate, cold images, with much snow – the eternal snows – and with no apparent sign of human life. Mr V stood before me, as though paralysed, benumbed, immobile. I asked him to sit down.

At one point he took a deep breath, and said: 'I love mountains, I love solitude . . .'. As I looked at the photos of the eternal snow and ice, he touched his head. I understood him to mean that he was feeling cold in the 'summit' of his own mountain, of his heavy rocky body. 'I'm not here for myself,' he said in a flat and inexpressive voice, 'but for the philosophy of my life and to clarify some of the visions I have. Dr T, from the Santa Giuliana clinic in Verona, sent me to you because he wanted your opinion as a specialist.'

He again fell silent, then seemed to realize I was waiting for him to go on. In a tone of voice bereft of all feeling, he told me that he worked as a lawyer, that he was 32, and that he found it hard to think and to concentrate, and to feel things. At that point, I saw him pull a face, as though in pain – as though he were trying desperately to put feelings and thoughts together. After a few moments, he said:

I find it very difficult to make contact with other people. You are the third psychoanalyst I have seen. The first time, it wasn't for me but for my sister. She became pregnant to a man who was not her fiancé; that made for problems with her real fiancé. He had had a terrible car accident which left him completely paralysed and impotent.

Mr V fell silent, a worried look on his face. Then he saw on my desk a little metal object. He asked if he could pick it up. He noticed it was a marine calendar.

35

'Yes,' I said, 'But I'm not too sure how to use it.' He then read the small print on the calendar, and said, 'This calendar goes from 1991 to 2040'. I was surprised, since I hadn't read that myself – the print was too small, so that I found it almost illegible. I had bought it in Paris near my consulting rooms, in a specialized shop which sells objects connected with the sea. I was more interested in the aesthetic and playful side, which took me back in fantasy to my imaginary trips to the South Pole; in my imaginary infantile world I was very interested in the fantastic adventures of Jules Verne. Perhaps that instrument could have belonged to Captain Nemo himself.

What for me was a nice toy, for Mr V was a great discovery. I said to him: 'You seem very curious about this calendar.' He replied: 'Yes. I am very concerned about problems of time – especially about the present and the future.' He said this with a pathetic smile on his face. Mr V always had a fixed look on his face, an inflexible expression, but just then he was very moving. He stirred up feelings of empathy and of sympathy in me. I could therefore contrast the heavy package of his gift with a lighter, more emotional kind of feeling, though these emotions were still very much enveloped in a cold wrapping.

His pregnant sister became a metaphor for his own heavy and distressing body package; his past weighed heavily on him and he required my help in order to bring it to life. Was I to be the right midwife for Mr V's anxiety? Could I help him come out into the open, to be born again? Would we both be able – in time – to create enough space and a warm climate in which delivery would go well? Or did he still need to be covered-up, wrapped-up in a package like his gift to me, contained and made well again in a package/hospital? He was petrified and frozen.

In order to find his truth, he had to climb to the top of the Himalayas – in fact, he went there on some kind of adventure trip, alone, for two weeks – and then go 'down below' to hell or at least to purgatory, to a psychoanalytic encounter with his unconscious. This Dante-like image made me think also of a text by a surrealist English writer and painter, Leonora Carrington, who wrote a novella called 'Down Below' (1944). As I was continuing my associations, I heard Mr V saying: 'I would very much like you to be with me all the time, so as to give me the answer'. He was asking me to come back from my distractions – but at the same time he was making me dream and escape, or perhaps asking me to meet him somewhere in our common dreaming illusory world (Resnik 2001b).

I remained silent, looking at him. This time, a pained expression crossed his brow and he half-closed his eyes. I felt he was about to cry, to thaw out. 'I have the feeling that myths are important to you,' I said.

'Myths are fantastic beliefs, visions about life,' he said. Then, with a catch in his voice, he went on: 'They're part of philosophy, perhaps a philosophy of the fantastic.' 'I'd be very interested to hear of your philosophy of the fantastic,' I said. I added that my comment about the importance for Mr V of myths came as I associated to the title of the book he gave me at the beginning of the session. '*Dolo-miti 360°*' made me think of *dolor* (pain) and *miti* (myths, in Italian) – something to do with a painful myth, one which could almost be seen in the expression on his face. Perhaps he needed me to make it less painful and more gentle. (In Italian, *mite* means 'gentle', 'moderate', 'temperate'.) Mr V's fantasy mythology and philosophy interested me. I commented: 'You are trying to communicate a very important message which weighs heavily on you, something which makes you feel all wrapped up, like the book. Your fantasy philosophy of life is a set of painful myths, perhaps.'

His unconscious 'mythological' preoccupations were therefore implicit in the message of the gift he had handed me. I was to understand his demands, help him open his personal 'package' and perhaps go through purgatory and hell with him. In the transference, I was to travel with him up and down, from the hills and mountains to the valleys of his unconscious, of his intimate geography, above all offering him a space in which to experiment with movement and life.

After a pause, Mr V said to me: 'I am afraid to feel my emotions, never mind express them'. 'I can see that in your eyes and in your voice,' I replied. 'Your pain is visible on your face from time to time, though the emotion it expresses sometimes is dissociated from the rest.'

'I need to protect myself with a solid covering.'

'Yes, and the package you brought was very solid. Maybe you don't feel very solid inside – too fragile and sensitive.'

At the end of the session, he expressed the wish to see me again: 'Will I have to wait long?' I looked in my personal calendar and said: 'Well, you will have to wait for a couple of weeks – but not until the year 2040'.

A few days later, I happened to meet Dr T, the psychiatrist who had referred the patient to me. He showed me a letter he had received from Mr V; on the envelope was written: '*Do not open, if possible, before 13 February 2004*' (these figures being a variation on 2040). In fact Dr T and myself – for reasons to do with our ages! – felt that we should not wait, so we opened the letter. Mr V had written about the future and about the pain which human beings feel; he thought that he ought to contribute to solving the question, perhaps through discovering some ideal medication or other. 'Human reasoning may prove faulty when something has to be done for the whole of humanity.' This made me think of a 360-degree perspective, as it were, going full circle, perhaps.

He added that he would like to be useful to humankind, especially to all those who were suffering like him. He mentioned the philosopher and epistemologist Karl Popper, who said (according to Mr V) that psychoanalysis was interesting but not scientific in the usual sense of the word. Mr V identified with Karl Popper – on several occasions he would be very critical of psychoanalysis – yet at the same time in his first session he showed that he wanted my help all the same.

37

Indeed, Mr V remained very present in my mind for several days after that first session. He managed to communicate a deep ontological and metaphysical feeling about existence and about history. In his anxiety over time, there seemed to be a very deeply buried preoccupation with death, related to his mental immobility and immutability – to his absence of vitality, in other words. My impression was that through his frozen mountains with their eternal snow-caps, he was expressing a perhaps grandiose feeling of eternity and perpetual immobility. His experience of living time was to a great extent paralysed, his heavy, melancholic body was blocked, and he needed help if he was to rediscover the rhythm of his life and its temporal dimension. I felt that his frozen body could all the same be helped to thaw out, though it might mean an apocalyptic avalanche once the snows began to melt.

Mr V told Dr T that he had spent a couple of weeks alone in the Himalayas. He had wanted to meet head-on the powerful and colossal immutability of the mountains which, with their eternal snows, defied the whole idea of the finitude of existence. He survived that extreme experience – thanks, perhaps, to his psychological glaciation.

Mr V had a religious belief about the mountains, a fetishism of Nature which seemed to be linked to those cultures which were concerned with the mythology of Nature. In the Sumerian civilization, in the era of polytheistic (pre-monotheistic) Semitic culture, all elements of Nature were personified by a *ba'al* or spirit – the spirit of the mountains, of the rivers, of vegetation, of storms, and so on. I learned also that the cult of the *ba'alim* involved human sacrifice.

But what was Mr V's intimate religious belief? This is what we are still trying to clarify together. He has been in treatment with me – with the support of Dr T and his clinic – for some years now. He has changed a great deal and has come back to life. But 'de-frozen', he is rather sad and at times depressed in a very moving way. At one point, he said: 'I'm coming back to life, and life is not completely dark – there is a little bit of grey. At times, I can even see the colours of nature, but at others I feel I am alone in a desert'.


## Conclusion

The four clinical cases discussed in this chapter dramatize certain aspects of bodily reality and bodily identifications in psychosis. At every new stage in life, it is difficult to integrate pain and distress; movement from one phase to another or from one space to another implies that what is being left behind has to be mourned. The body image changes during the mourning process in accordance with the unconscious fantasies which are linked to every separation or transformation that occurs in one's life.

It is not by mere chance that the onset of psychosis often has its roots in puberty and adolescence, *the* great somatic and psychological transformation of life. If we are to think about bodily identifications in psychosis, we have to develop our understanding of the language of the body. For my part, I am conscious of the fact that our body 'talks' to us and that our unconscious fantasies are expressed in that way too. Throughout my many years of clinical experience, I have been able to make contact with autistic children and psychotic adults through what they express through their body. As I have pointed out, the body is living memory. Gestures, facial expressions, wrinkles and everything else which goes to make up our *persona*-mask are manifestations of the traces left by our personal history.

In the transference, psychotic or non-psychotic, making empathic contact with the meaning and substance of fantasy takes us back to the earliest experiences of our childhood: cold/warm, dry/wet, hard/soft, full/empty. These elementary sensations in both patient and analyst – this 'body to body' encounter – are part of the climate of the analytical experience; this is what I call the 'ecology of the transference'.

Between 'to be' and 'not to be', a clinical meandering along the psychotic pathways of the body becomes manifest in the transference. As they become aware of the substance or matter of the body – iron body, petrified body, frozen body – analyst and patient endeavour to understand what will become of the fantasies which inhabit it. Not only is there projection outside of the self, but also there may be a projection into the self, an internal projection – the vicissitudes of projective identification and its transformations 'within' the reality of the body.

After discussing transmission and learning, then, in this chapter, the realities of the body in psychosis, I want now to make contact with the body of my own psychoanalytic history. The next chapter therefore focuses on my first encounter with psychosis in an institutional setting. At that time, I was working in two different contexts: in private practice with patients in individual analysis, and in a psychiatric clinic with patients in group analysis. It is this experience which I would now like to share with the reader.

# 3

# The Role of the Body in Psychosis:
# A group experience

In this chapter, I discuss my earliest psychoanalytic experience with a group of chronic psychotic patients. The therapeutic group began in 1950, in a psychiatric hospital in Buenos Aires. Raul Usandivaras was the motive force behind this innovative experience. At the time, there were several of us young psychiatrists, all in analysis, working in the unit headed by Professor Eduardo Krapf. Professor Krapf was a psychoanalyst and professor of psychiatry first in Germany then in Buenos Aires. (I was to meet him again in Geneva in 1955, where he was director of psychiatric research with the World Health Organization.) Raul Usandivaras was enthusiastic about an article Paul Schilder had written in 1939, 'Results and Problems of Group Psychotherapy in Severe Neuroses', and he wanted to do some research work with a group of chronic psychotic patients who had lived for some time in an institutional setting. He asked me to work with him, then invited Juan Morgan to join us. For a period of six months in the late 1940s Juan Morgan had participated in Bion's experiences with groups at the Tavistock Clinic in London. Raul Usandivaras and I were fortunate to be able to work with him and so benefit from what he could communicate to us of Bion's teaching.

We chose ten or so patients in the unit, all of whom had been hospitalized for many years. The hospital itself was an old asylum, so that we could quite easily follow the daily life of the patients either in the unit itself or in the grounds; in a certain sense, the patients were destined to remain there for the rest of their life. They were to all intents and purposes 'frozen' and emotionally 'cut-off'. One year into the experiment, we presented a preliminary report on our work to a psychiatric congress in Tucuman, Argentina. Later, I published a paper of my own based on the experience, first in the Argentine *Revista de Psicoanálisis* and, some years later, in French. The present chapter is an updated and more complete version of those papers.

In the history of group psychoanalysis in Argentina, the work we did was the first of its kind to be attempted there. I had already worked with psychotic patients in individual analysis under the guidance of Pichon-Rivière; this new experience allowed me to complete my training and benefit from a more global view of the issues involved. Ever since I had begun thinking about psychosis and working with psychotic patients, I was struck by the way their body seemed to be the vehicle for expressing themselves. I realized how difficult it was for them to use ordinary language as a means of expression. Often gestures, grimaces, the look in their eyes made communication meaningful in a way that ordinary words did not; either they could not speak or else they would use bizarre and repetitive phrases as a kind of sound barrier to protect themselves. These neologisms, of course, were meaningful in themselves, but at that time I was not always able to decipher them correctly. What also was important for me was the atmosphere or 'climate' which was created in the transference – I already had the idea that these psychotic patients were capable of establishing a transference. I remember how Pichon-Rivière, my mentor in this kind of approach, used to say: 'You know, these patients with a long institutional past behind them, they are virginal as far as communication is concerned. But that does not mean that they cannot communicate.' He was as surprised as I was at times when he succeeded in making contact, sometimes spontaneously, with schizophrenic patients presenting highly autistic defences. That helped me to understand that what is sometimes called 'spontaneous recovery' is in fact an unexpected opening-up of the psychotic patient's healthy part (unsullied by any form of contact – virginal), enabling the patient to wake up. When I talk of waking up, this is because in my view these patients are mentally asleep; they experience everyday reality as if it were a dream.

Thus, just as in dreams, it is normal for them to hallucinate reality. Bion said that, in the transference, psychotic patients never know whether they are asleep or awake. I think of this state as being a development of the work of the trans-ference. For me, generally speaking, chronic psychotic patients are constantly dreaming the real world without being able to wake up from their dream. If they wake up as daylight dawns, they find themselves faced with the choice between life and death. One of my recent patients, Silvano (who is of Italian extraction), a schizophrenic patient who has spent the past few years locked up in his apartment, managed to communicate with me via the drawing he made of an apparently dead soldier dating from the time of Charlemagne. I understood him to mean that he was the soldier, 'dead tired' after years of struggling with the opposing forces which were inside him. For many a long session, military personnel and church officials (hallucinated objects) 'accompanied' us in our work together.

One day he said to me: 'There are just the two of us here.' I understood him to mean that he was wakening up from his hallucinatory world. After that session, Silvano's appetite returned and he decided to have a hamburger on the

41

Boulevard St Michel. On another occasion, when he was feeling sad, he told me he had eaten a pancake (*crêpe*, in French). I asked him what the word *crêpe* made him think of; '*Crepare*,' he answered (a colloquial term in Italian meaning 'to die'). His dilemma then was whether to waken up to life – by no means easy for him – or to go back to being a dead soldier. To feel himself alive was too powerful a sensation for him; I had an image of him walking pitifully along the Boulevard St Michel holding a hamburger in one hand and a pancake in the other.

The experience I want to relate now was also for me, in my own journey through life, a significant moment for my thinking about and research into the field of psychosis.

## The semantics of the body

For long, the body was believed to be opposed to the soul. Whereas the monistic and spiritualist conception of medieval scholasticism laid claim to a clear and reflexive consciousness and its 'rights' over the *corpus delicti*, the Cartesian *res extensa* opened up consciousness to the reality of the human body. That was how Descartes made use of Aristotle's ideas on the semiological reality of the living body: the body is a sign – *semeion* – of the presence of the soul, and the soul is that of bodily presence. Cartesian reflective ambiguity – which is not ambivalence – reintroduces the truth of the body. The idea of opposition between body and soul may be expressed in pathological terms as a psychotic dissociation: here, the manifestations of dualism are particularly extensive.

The depersonalized patient's 'spirit' is not aware of what his or her body is doing: the body is an other. Such patients smile for no apparent reason, their movements are mechanical and their 'mannerisms' seem to be divorced from anything else they may be doing.

I have spent many years treating psychotic patients in several different contexts and I have made a particular study of group dynamics in the therapeutic approach. When a group of long-stay patients is brought together, their behaviour is a prime subject for observation; it is also an excellent occasion for communicating, for trying to understand the meaning of their various gestures and movements and for assessing the existential climate of the group as a whole. In psychotic patients, disorders of symbolic processes mean that words or phrases are not of a different nature from gestures. Moreover, their body language is rich in meaningful allusions which they cannot put into words.

My counter-transference experience and the knowledge I acquired in the course of this work as co-therapist and participant observer during the three years the group lasted in the 1950s taught me a great deal about the importance of body language. A living body always contains infantile implications in the sense of the ability to play with and make use of bodily messages. All adults keep within themselves to some extent an infantile mode of relating, and traces of this can be found in some of their specific or idiosyncratic behaviour patterns. These specific patterns enable us to recognize a language which belongs both to the past and to the present, one which is flexible in its modes of expression. We all carry along with us our own personal history as it is inscribed in our body; above all it is the child within us who recalls and expresses our basic anxieties, either directly or in some roundabout way.

An a-historical approach to transference synchrony – from a phenomeno-logical point of view – highlights its implicit diachronic dimension. The idea is to decipher and to understand the synchrony of the signifiers.

What is usually called a person's 'character' consists in a more or less coherent or specific set of signifiers inscribed in his or her physical body; these define the individual as a living *persona* (mask). Generally speaking, in schizophrenia, these various features fail to connect together in an integrated harmonious whole. The schizophrenic gives the impression of not being a whole person, of not being an individual in the etymological sense of the term ('not divided') – a more or less discordant conglomerate would perhaps be an appropriate image, since the fragments of the patient's personality cannot succeed in organizing themselves into a coherent whole. It is for this reason that Bion spoke of the schizophrenic as a group-personality, a set of fragments which are not in communicative contact with one another.

Group dynamics is one way of studying language through its various poly-morphous and polysemous modes of expression. The group situation itself acts as a stimulus; it is one way of waking up after a long sleep. In psychotic patients, disorders of communication and needs are mainly expressed through gestures and the style of body posture – their manner of being, as it were. The presence of other people's bodies in the group acts as an important stimulus coming from the everyday reality of the surrounding world. The reality principle does not prevent acknowledging that some things are 'unreal' – including perhaps one's own reality. The reality principle is also a matter of principle. We all of us – whatever the state of our health – have principles with respect to what reality is or is not. When the petrified body of the chronically ill psychotic patient begins to 'thaw out', the system of mutual interactions and the transference – the experience of exchanging – also start to appear. When time begins to march forward again after having stood still for so long, it feels as though something painful, distressing and hard to tolerate is opening up.

A brief gesture in someone's direction is already the expression of a wish, a need, a painful feeling or an intentionality which remains to be fleshed out and deciphered. Bodily expressions are a means of signifying the modalities in which time is awakening inside the patient's body and the manner in which interactions with other people can take place. The degree of fluidity (or, *a contrario*, viscosity) of introjection and projection indicates how expressive the patient's language is and what stage it has reached. Starting from this kind of interaction, materialized through the body's gestures and perhaps words, a network of social relationships can be organized. This is what Foulkes (1964) calls the group matrix. This network is dynamic in structure and enables the group to develop its capacity for communicating and for transmitting messages along the different lines of communication which the group possesses. The American term is 'channels of communication', and in family therapy this relational network would be called a systemic approach to the clinical and theoretical material.

I would now like to illustrate these points in a little more detail with reference to the clinical group experience I had in Argentina. As I said, the group was 'headed' by co-therapists, one of whom was a participant observer; that colleague, sitting by my side, took notes during the sessions and, afterwards, we discussed these and completed them. The group itself lasted for several years and gave me my first experience with this kind of technique; I was at that time already interested in and working on some ideas concerning various kinds of approach with psychotic patients in a group context.

For someone actually to say something was quite an event – usually silence, in all of its phenomenological dimensions, reigned: shut off, tense, fluid, viscous, sometimes more open, overwhelming, condescending. Different bodily expressions indicated the importance of the *locus* of the patient's body with respect to the role played by his or her corporality as an extension of the inner self. In this attempt to report one session, I shall try to illustrate some modalities and 'manners of being' which are specific to the body and verbal language (the 'body of speech') which the groups members used.

The session took place in the morning. My colleague Raul Usandivaras and I were a few minutes late in arriving. There was a short silence at first while we all looked at one another quizzically, then one of the patients said 'Good evening', staring at us as he did so with an expression which was tense and yet almost couldn't-care-less at the same time. Another group member came up to me, a sheet of paper in his hand; a few lines were scribbled on it. The patient wanted me to read his message, then he sat back down. A third patient, whom I shall call Mr B, through clenched teeth and with his body held rigid, muttered something that I could not quite catch. I had the impression he was trying to tell us a story. His lips pronounced, with difficulty, a few syllables which obviously had little to do with his body language (which was static, really). I did, however, manage to catch a few words: 'brother . . . abandoned . . . dear . . .'. Mr B was simultaneously moving his hands about in a way that expressed discontent and loneliness.

Since most of the other group members were paying close attention to him, I decided to take his message as if he were the spokesperson expressing the group's frustration at having had to wait for us to arrive. That uncomfortable situation had already been hinted at by the patient who had greeted us with a 'Good evening' rather than a 'Good morning'.

44

The group was still impatient, but henceforth for a different reason. It was no longer a matter of waiting for the doctors to arrive; the patients themselves were locked in a struggle, expressed on an infantile level, over who could attract the attention of the group 'leaders'. They began to express their personal wishes, each in his or her own way – muttering, gesticulating, writing down words – while others waited anxiously but hopefully, and attempting to attract our attention through gestures. This kind of attitude expressed an anxiety which was oral in nature.

A few minutes later, another patient commented that, when Mr B spoke, his words were confused and inaudible – whereas, if he had put them into song, as he usually did, it would have been much easier to understand him. The patient added that, when Mr B sang, he probably felt it easier to express his feelings – whereas, when he spoke, his words sounded hollow and 'soul-less'. I tried to explain that, when Mr B sang, his words were no longer hollow because he could put some 'soul' into them; this helped him get in touch with his feelings and express them spontaneously, not in his usual cold detached manner. When Mr B spoke, his words seemed to lack feeling and have no warmth to them. Mr B, however, was still murmuring 'brother . . . abandoned . . .'; I added that sometimes the words he uttered were full of resentment as regards this 'dear brother' of his. It was obvious that he felt abandoned by his brother in the psychiatric unit – and when I arrived late for our session together it was as though I were abandoning the group.

## The symbolic order and its deficiencies

It has often been said that psychotics use symbols to express themselves – their words, however, are mostly frozen, and all 'space' between the thing perceived (the primary object) and its representation (the secondary object) is flattened. The *loci* of signified and signifier are superimposed one on the other, so that everything becomes indistinguishable and concrete. Thinking, in such cases, becomes a gestural behaviour which only imitates thinking – a psychopathic form of thinking rather than an abstract and symbolic cognitive process. Words are no longer genuine abstractions, they are concrete objects. The idea of concrete thinking in psychotic patients is familiar to classical psychiatry. Hanna Segal (1957) has explored the issues involved when, as in psychosis, symbol formation is modified. She describes what she calls a *symbolic equation* in which the symbol becomes the equivalent of a deed, a material object or a concrete action. Personally, I prefer to distinguish three stages; concrete thinking, proto-symbolic thinking, and true symbolic thinking; for me, then, the symbolic equation is a proto–symbolic equivalent.

In Mr B's case, for example, to give verbal expression to his resentment at having been abandoned and at not having his demands met would really be, for him, a concretely dangerous *act*. He produced words as if they were things which could damage reality in some way – therefore, they had to be kept under control in order to protect reality from his angry feelings. When his lips tightened as he spoke, they were acting like a sphincter controlling the projection or expulsion of word-things (oral anality). What the other patient felt as 'soul-less' words was the result of the emotional depersonalization of speech followed by an evacuation out of the sphere of thought – projected either into Mr B's body (gestures or somatization) or into some other object in the patient's immediate surroundings. Singing was an attempt at sublimating these painful feelings of resentment into something more abstract and potentially less harmful, with the aim of re-creating or repairing his lost world. Mourning the loss of affective cathexes and object relations implies the need to repair any damage done and to restore the object.

## A body in pain

At one point, Mr A, another member of the group, began to talk about physical illness. 'Some patients complain that they feel pain and that their bodies are changing; they consult doctors and ask them for injections.' I commented that, in addition to expressing itself via words, music and written messages, the group was communicating its anxiety, pain and feelings of physical torment. Injections implied the need for immediate relief through a concrete act.

Disorders of thinking and of emotionality were turning into real physical phenomena – or perhaps they were being defensively displaced on to the body and its various organs: the hypochondriacal solution. The dissociation between body and soul, body and thought or body and mind was in the service of defending the patient (or group) against psychotic anxiety. Though there was here the image of a body which was unwell, there were also more positive signs of a wish for recovery.

## An atmosphere of emptiness

The physical body always has some involvement with thinking. As Mr A was talking, he was fiddling with an empty lunch-box which he brought along to every session as though it were an integral part of his body schema. Once I had realized that, in the group context, it corresponded to an underlying feeling of emptiness, I could see the lunch-box/sign as the expression of what the group was experiencing: a common denominator signifying that the atmosphere in the group had to do with a depopulated reality, stripped of all life, an emptiness which had to be filled.

This was not simply an oral need for satisfaction but also a deeper feeling which was more metaphysical in nature. It was an existential feeling, an experience of emptiness which manifested itself through the body and was represented in schematic form by the lunch-box. For me, this was the group's basic fantasy. When I offered them that interpretation, the group fell silent. No one spoke for some time, then Mr A began to ask questions of my colleague (as participant observer, Dr Usandivaras did not actually speak during the sessions)[1] and of me: 'How many people have you cured here? Can you cure cancer and syphilis? What microbe causes that?'

Another patient spoke of 'the moment of death' and Mr B began singing softly: 'Brothers, if the doctor could be mine, mine . . .'. I interpreted the representation which the group members had of their illness – something terrifying like cancer or syphilis. That representation expressed both their despair and their wish to be cured; they seemed, nonetheless, to feel that no cure was possible given the extremely serious nature of the illness evoked. I am convinced that in every psychotic patient, no matter how chronically ill, there is a part of the self which hopes for recovery in spite of all the despair. Obviously the evocation of cancer and syphilis had to do with the group's fantasy of the seriousness of their state of health.

At that point, a patient who until then had remained silent – his attempts to say anything were always either incoherent or metaphorical – said: 'Blessed be the cancer of our body which cures the cancer of our soul!' That state-ment highlighted what I believe to be a typical fantasy where mental illness is concerned. It is experienced not only as a 'cancer of the soul', but also as a dissociative defence which displaces the soul cancer on to and into the body in order to preserve the soul. Here the patients realized that dissociation led only to a false recovery which left the root causes of the illness untouched; they wanted to understand how their illness had taken hold and to discover the 'microbes' which had generated it.

It was interesting also to observe how another member of the group – more regressed than the others, he was nicknamed 'Baby' – managed to express himself through body language and very infantile gestures and movements; in other words, he was expressing the rest of the group's most primitive and elementary feelings. 'Baby' seemed to have little interest in what had been transpiring since the beginning of the session; he looked more and more like a shy little child, hiding his face in the folds of his arms. Since the other group members looked at him a great deal, my impression was that he was the spokesperson for the group's regressive and infantile anxieties and reveries.

Later, two patients loudly demanded help and affection from my colleague and myself. One said: 'We want a bit of bread'. I felt this attempt at coming closer to be very intense on the part of the group. The patients were expressing them-selves so powerfully and demandingly that, in my counter-transference, I had the impression that they were starving babies who wanted to have mother all to themselves, ready to suck her dry. In my interpretation, I added that my colleague and I were to some extent representative of the group mother – the two breasts which they were demanding so insistently and excitedly. Together we were a maternal part-object (breast-mother) which was being fought over by all those who wanted a part of what we could give.

Just then, one patient, extremely excited, not to say beside himself, argued that what I had just said was 'a nightmare which had suddenly fallen on the group'. After a few seconds, he went on: 'Right now, everything seems like it's a dream, a courageous dream, exciting and disturbing, one which is wakening up a group of sleeping people and upsetting them.' (At that time, I had already the intuitive idea that one of the existential characteristics of chronic psychotics was the impression that they were asleep or potentially dead.)

I was aware of the anxiety which was in the group, and I tried to explain that my comments may well have fallen on the group like a nightmare. That 'night-mare' had suddenly pulled them out of their state of almost constant lethargy, proof that their lives had been dormant for such a long time. My comment seemed to bring some relief to the group. Another patient stared at my co-therapist and said: 'Once upon a time, a she-wolf was feeding her two cubs'; he looked at my colleague's brown jacket, describing it as 'woven from a beautiful dream'. I understood him to mean that the she-wolf, a primitive image found in fairy tales, was personified by my colleague representing the idealized image of the good mother who has been found again, a truly beautiful dream, a truly beautiful breast.

Most of the group members were staring at my colleague and trying to get closer to this she-wolf/mother. This idealized image of the maternal figure stood in stark contrast to the persecutory image which I personified (the bad breast). At first, my attitude was felt to be harmful; I represented a clear and blinding reality which their eyes suddenly contemplated, in contrast to the oneiric world of delusion from which they had been dragged – that world then took on the appearance of a nightmare.

According to Klein (1952), 'the idealized breast forms the corollary of the persecuting breast; and in so far as idealization is derived from the need to be protected from persecuting objects, it is a method of defence against anxiety' (Klein 1975 [1952]: 64). That sentence may sometimes give the impression that idealization is pathological; in fact, it is rather the exaggeration of a normal phenomenon which we find in relationships of warmth, friendship and love. In 1958, I had tea with Mrs Klein in her house; Elliott Jaques was there too (she was very attached to him at that time). His ideas on Klein's conception of social systems and organizations are highly relevant here (Jaques 1955).

The orality of this particular group was intense; they expressed their infan-tile voracity via the fantasy of sucking the breast dry and emptying it of all substance. This oral demand reappeared later, when one of the patients said: 'All babies want both breasts just for themselves.' In that statement, the patient was

48

expressing how difficult it is to share the source of goodness and the underlying resentment everyone feels at not having taken possession of the mother's body in its totality. In this respect, the group's anxiety was alternately paranoid and depressive, depending on the circumstances – the feeling that the mother had been lost as a result of the projection of the group's own destructive oral impulses on to the object, or the group's preoccupation with recovering and restoring a good relationship with the maternal figure. Fairy tales are a way of reactivating the mythical time of a primal experience.

The group tried to dramatize the reparation of the loved maternal object by means of a kind of polymorphous ritual made up of songs, gestures and speech; the aim of this was to re-create an ideal era – a golden age, the age of fairy tales.

I tried to describe the ritual to the members of the group, pointing out the different modes of expression and taking the opportunity to emphasize one particular aspect: one of the patients who had said nothing at all until then began 'talking' in a mainly bodily way – he seemed to be very tense and downcast. As I watched him, he began by saying that people who had cancer or syphilis were of no concern to him and that he could not understand why he was in hospital. All he knew was that his wife was unfaithful to him, that he himself was jealous and that everybody seemed to be accusing him of something and making fun of him. I replied that perhaps he had the impression that I hadn't observed him very much since the beginning of the session and that I hadn't paid much attention to him – in other words, that I had been 'unfaithful' to him, just as his wife had been. Moreover, he imagined that I and the rest of the group were making fun of him – perhaps that explained why he was feeling so tense and dejected. The patient retorted that he was feeling quite all right – not like the other members of the group: they were crazy, and the nursing staff were bizarre and kept on tormenting him. He concluded his remarks with: 'They persecute me here just as my wife used to.'

After a pause – which I took care to 'observe' – I pointed out that the group was trying to come to terms with its 'cancer of the soul' in two ways. On the one hand, they were trying to see the group illness as being part of each one of them – an illness (cancer or syphilis) which involved a highly destructive component. On the other hand, thanks to the mediation of the patient who had just spoken, they wanted to deny the existence of that feeling of sickness inside themselves – pushing it outside was a way of getting rid of it. Illness seemed to be something which did not concern them directly, yet it embarrassed them – it was always other people who were ill, not them. Projection of this sort is in widespread use as a defence mechanism in psychotic patients with pronounced paranoid trends. In the first of these two situations, the individual is unhappy but more in touch with his or her state of (ill-)health; in the second, the illness is projected outside and is therefore ignored.

## Discussion

Rereading something I wrote almost fifty years previously takes on the character of an evocative dialogue with myself. I recognize my own style of expression and find myself in touch with how I still approach the question of psychosis. At the time, it was quite a novel experience for me, and a very interesting one; I was able to fix in my mind many aspects of the psychotic patient's language and speech patterns in a group situation. Deep anxiety is usually expressed in some physical (bodily) way or other, or through objects which have some connection with the body (the lunch-box, for example). What the group has to say goes further than that, of course – there are changes and structural fluctuations in the network of relations which in themselves are a form of coded language, the importance of which cannot be ignored. It is expressed, for instance, in the group atmosphere, through its behaviour and spatial changes, in the contours of the 'group body' and the shape of its 'organs'. Each member functions at one point or another as a group 'organ' – the idea of the group-as-organism or body schema (Schilder 1950). Thanks to the in-depth work done in the group, the different members may, over time, become aware of this body schema. As regards the relationship between the surrounding space and the atmosphere of the group, Schilder's chapter on the sociology of the body image is particularly relevant here; the author writes:

> But objects which were once connected with the body always retain something of the quality of the body-image on them . . . The voice, the breath, the odour, faeces, menstrual blood, urine, semen, are still parts of the body-image even when they are separated in space from the body (Cf Roheim) . . . the space in and around the postural model is not the space of physics. The body-image incorporates objects or spreads itself into space.
>
> (Schilder 1950: 213)

Bringing together the members of the group for each session is the equivalent of re-membering, a memory which is part of the history which is worked over during the psychoanalytic process.

Commenting, observing and interpreting are interventions which put me in the position of a semiologist/psychoanalyst. Once deciphered, the signs which appear in what the group expresses help us to understand the material evoked in the session, as well as the unconscious grammar and syntax the group uses. The signs of this language, which mainly refer back to very primitive fantasies, are imprinted on the body of the group as a whole and on the body of each of its members. The *locus* or extension of each participant's body highlights a particular dimension which, given its place in the network, acquires meaning as a spatial sign or signal. For example, the person whom the rest of the group called 'Baby' took it upon himself, by expressing what he had to say exclusively

50

through gestures, to represent the most infantile aspect of the group, the one which had to be as close as possible to the group leader – the maternal figure as a source of everything that was good. The most paranoid member – the patient who said that the nursing staff were all crazy – sat as far away as possible from the rest of us. This was his way of expressing the distance between the part of the group heavily cathected with a persecutory content and the possibility of communicating any of this to the rest of us.

## Conclusion

My work with autistic children and psychotic adults has taught me a great deal. I am convinced that the therapist's main role is to serve as an intermediary between body (non-verbal thinking) and mind. The 'therapist-leader' has to be sensitive to everything which is going on, in the psychotic and in the non-psychotic universe. The dialectics between these two aspects must never be forgotten; the analyst has to come to terms with the mental and physical problems which he or she may encounter as a result of the transference/counter-transference situation (nowadays, I would be more inclined to speak of the double transference). The psychoanalyst is an 'ethnologist of the unconscious', whose vocation is to solve the mysteries of the unexpected and the unknown.

The proto-history of diachrony is expressed through the spatial and a-historical synchrony of the transference phenomena. Everything which participates in the history of the group appears topographically as a living geography which evolves in accordance with the vicissitudes of the analytical encounter. Basically, it is not a question of the semiology or psychoanalysis of the patient, but of the encounter itself (Resnik et al. 1982).

I am convinced that more in-depth research into this kind of experience would prove helpful for those who are particularly motivated not only by the institutional aspects linked to social psychiatry but also by contemporary ideas on the practice of psychoanalysis.

What the group situation adds to individual psychoanalysis in addition to the dramatization of the unconscious is the presence of a third party – public opinion. This aspect of the group-individual analytic space could be related to a stage presentation of a Greek tragedy in which the Chorus is not only a supplementary actor (Aristotle's thesis) but also the presence of the audience on the stage (this is what I mean by 'public opinion').

Reading that pioneer experience once again is like a journey through time for me. I think there is a kind of reciprocal movement along the temporal axis of my personal biography, which allows me to be on the stage of my debut while at the same time enabling me to develop in the present a dialogue with the various 'stages' and phases of my life.

# 4

# The Universe of Madness:
# Frozen words and thoughts[1]

*In memory of my mentor and friend, Georges Daumézon*

## An experience with long-stay psychotic patients in the Sainte-Anne Hospital, Paris

When we were at sea, junketing, tippling, discoursing, and telling stories, Pantagruel rose and stood up to look out; then asked us, Do you hear nothing, gentlemen? Methinks I hear some people talking in the air, yet I can see nobody. Hark! According to his command we listened, and with full ears sucked in the air as some of you suck oysters, to find if we could hear some sound scattered through the sky; and to lose none of it, like the Emperor Antoninus some of us laid their hands hollow next to their ears; but all this would not do, nor could we hear any voice. Yet Pantagruel continued to assure us he heard various voices in the air, some of men, and some of women.

At last we began to fancy that we also heard something, or at least that our ears tingled; and the more we listened, the plainer we discerned the voices, so as to distinguish articulate sounds. This mightily frightened us, and not without cause; since we could see nothing, yet heard such various sounds and voices of men, women, children, horses, &c., insomuch that Panurge cried out, Cods-belly, there is no fooling with the devil; we are all beshit, let's fly. There is some ambuscado hereabouts. Friar John, art thou here my love? I pray thee, stay by me, old boy. Hast thou got thy swindging tool? See that it do not stick in thy scabbard; thou never scourest it half as it should be. We are undone. Hark! They are guns, gad judge me. Let's fly, I do not say with hands

52

and feet, as Brutus said at the battle of Pharsalia; I say, with sails and oars. Let's whip it away. I never find myself to have a bit of courage at sea; in cellars and elsewhere I have more than enough. Let's fly and save our bacon. I do not say this for any fear that I have; for I dread nothing but danger, that I don't; I always say it that shouldn't. The free archer of Baignolet said as much. Let us hazard nothing, therefore, I say, lest we come off bluely. Tack about, helm a-lee, thou son of a bachelor. Would I were now well in Quinquenais, though I were never to marry. Haste away, let's make all the sail we can. They'll be too hard for us; we are not able to cope with them; they are ten to our one, I'll warrant you. Nay, and they are on their dunghill, while we do not know the country. They will be the death of us. We'll lose no honour by flying. Demosthenes saith that the man that runs away may fight another day. At least let us retreat to the leeward. Helm a-lee; bring the main-tack aboard, haul the bowlines, hoist the top-gallants. We are all dead men; get off, in the devil's name, get off.

Pantagruel, hearing the sad outcry which Panurge made, said, Who talks of flying? Let's first see who they are; perhaps they may be friends. I can discover nobody yet, though I can see a hundred miles round me. But let's consider a little. I have read that a philosopher named Petron was of opinion that there were several worlds that touched each other in an equilateral triangle; in whose centre, he said, was the dwelling of truth; and that the words, ideas, copies, and images of all things past and to come resided there; round which was the age; and that with success of time part of them used to fall on mankind like rheums and mildews, just as the dew fell on Gideon's fleece, till the age was fulfilled.

I also remember, continued he, that Aristotle affirms Homer's words to be flying, moving, and consequently animated. Besides, Antiphanes said that Plato's philosophy was like words which, being spoken in some country during a hard winter, are immediately congealed, frozen up, and not heard; for what Plato taught young lads could hardly be understood by them when they were grown old. Now, continued he, we should philosophize and search whether this be not the place where those words are thawed.

Rabelais, *Gargantua and Pantagruel*, Book Four, Chapter LV, 'How Pantagruel, being at sea, heard various unfrozen words'

In Book Four of *Gargantua and Pantagruel*, François Rabelais (1483–1553) raises the fundamental problem of frozen time. In 1538, Rabelais wrote his enchanting account of the sea voyages of Panurge and Pantagruel, a book which I found particularly inspiring as I was writing this chapter. In Chapter LV of Book Four, entitled 'How Pantagruel, being at sea, heard various unfrozen words', he relates how, as he was travelling to the North Pole, Pantagruel suddenly heard noises and voices in the air – the voices of men and of women, and the whinnying of horses. He then heard cannon being fired, as though some invisible battle was going on around them. He was frightened by these unexpected phenomena, appearing as out of thin air, in the midst of such a vast expanse of sea, so quiet and solitary. He told his fellow sailors what he thought was happening. Had they heard the same things as he had?

The answer was first in the negative, then in the affirmative. The other crew members, listening as hard as they could, finally admitted that they did indeed hear voices and noises scattered throughout the air. Their first reaction was to run away from the danger. One sailor said: 'They're going to kill us! Let's get out of here!' Pantagruel asked:

> Who is that runaway? Let us see first of all who these people are. I can't see anybody for a hundred miles around. Hush, listen! I read that a philosopher called Petron believed in a plurality of worlds which were tangent to one another, forming an equilateral triangle, in the centre of which rose the Dwelling of Truth. Here, there are words, ideas, models and presentations of anything belonging to the past or to the future.

Pantagruel went on to quote Aristotle, for whom Homer's words were fluttering about, flying around in the air and animated – almost as if they had a soul. 'Antiphanes spoke of frozen wintry words which change into ice when they come into contact with the freezing air; as a result, they can no longer be heard.'

In the following chapter, the pilot says:

> Be not afraid, my lord; we are on the confines of the Frozen Sea, on which, about the beginning of last winter, happened a great and bloody fight between the Arimaspians and the Nephelibates. Then the words and cries of men and women, the hacking, slashing, and hewing of battle-axes, the shocking, knocking, and jolting of armours and harassments, the neighing of horses, and all other martial din and noise, froze in the air; and now, the rigour of the winter being over, by the succeeding serenity and warmth of the weather they melt and are heard.

## A voyage to the North Pole

After that illuminating lesson by Rabelais on 'frozen words' in the course of Pantagruel's journey to the North Pole, I would like now to recount the vicissitudes of a psychoanalytic adventure in many ways reminiscent of that epic narrative.

It began in December 1980, with a group of long-stay patients, some of whom had been in the unit since 1960 or 1965. In my discussion, I shall illustrate some of my views on the individual self, the group self, and the psychotic self (Bion 1957). Bion differentiates between the psychotic and non-psychotic parts of the personality. In his work with groups, at times he would see the group as a 'self' and his interpretations were always directed to the group, not to individual members. In my approach, I do not restrict myself to group interpretations, because I feel that the group is not always an organized self. The disorganization and dispersion brought about by psychosis becomes a pathological ideology in conflict with the organizing and integrative tendencies of the group as a self. 'Attacks on linking' (Bion 1959) are already present here.

The group weighed anchor on a Friday morning at 11.30 in a very narrow room, almost a corridor, of the Sainte-Anne Hospital in Paris, on the first floor of the Henri-Rousselle Institute. The launch of this particular *Ship of Fools* was laborious, to say the least. Each stage of our voyage brought us together for one and a half hours. The medical director of the unit was present, together with three observers. Our initial idea was to experience with these psychotic patients a dramatic transference (or, perhaps, lack of transference) which might prove difficult to withstand – and to understand.

The members of the group were immobile and strange-looking. They saw me as an intruder into their personal world, a world without motion or e-motion. A cold, frozen world, sometimes shaken by unconnected gestures, mechanical and fragmented. For those patients, it was I who was bizarre, who came to wake them up, prepared to travel with them into their space and no doubt interfere with their petrified conception of the world.

At one point one of the male patients, Claude, said: 'I am a penguin'. I understood that to be the group's way of introducing me to how they experienced themselves – as an animal which lived far away: not a person, but a bird unable to fly, one which is ungainly and inarticulate. I looked at the rest of the group which was then being born for me (as I was probably, though I was not sure of the fact, being born for them). In a dyadic context, the birth of the transference is a double birth; in a group context it is a multiple birth.

I saw before me strange, frozen 'beings'. The narrowness of the room made me feel that they were inside a uterus or vagina, a vagina which did not allow them to move very much. Beside the 'penguin' sat Annie, dressed in furs and wearing a fur hat – she looked like an Eskimo. She too was immobile. In some ways she resembled an igloo rather than a person. There was something pathetic about her – living in the frost while protecting herself against the cold. She symbolized for me the mental and physical state of the group: immobilization, autistic protection, a state of being and living in a space far removed from ordinary time and space. Claude and Annie, through the way in which they introduced me to the group, were metaphorical images of what I could think of as the basic personality of the group (Kardiner 1945) and its basic assumptions;

the environment as a social mask-*persona*, the outer expression of an inner state in which all sentient beings were petrified. Basic personality is not synonymous with basic assumption but is related to it in the sense that it is the personification of a basic, unconscious desire or belief of the group. Basic assumption has, for Bion, a restrictive sense for psychotic patients. The more regressive the group, the more their need for dependency, protection and nourishment (material and spiritual); however, in the delusional transference, their needs are more specific and usually far removed from reality. Here, for example, Claude and Annie seemed to be in what Bion called a *pairing* B-A group, built upon the Oedipal myth – the group expects the ideal couple to produce a baby-Messiah which will lead to its salvation.

Psychotic patients are often polarized people, they feel either extreme cold or extreme heat; during their acute psychotic crisis, for example, they appear to be on fire. Time – the experience of living time – is blocked and reified. Symmetry is an expression of identity without diversity; catatonic patients are usually in a state of petrification.

Looking back at the group – though at that point it was an agglomeration or series of discrete beings rather than a real group – I could see a young woman patient, Dominique, a sort of adolescent troubadour of the Middle Ages (it was in some ways difficult to say whether Dominique was male or female), who said in a mixture of arrogance and pain: 'We cannot get out. We mad people have no place outside. We have a place here – here is where we can be mad.' But looking at them almost suffocating in that narrow corridor, I said to them: 'Well, you don't seem very happy here either.'

Dominique was sitting opposite Claude and Annie and her remarks seemed to wake them up. Claude-penguin started to move his right leg in a regular and rhythmical way, saying: 'When are we going to eat?' The newborn child coming in from the cold was impatient for something to eat.

From a frosty, immobile world, rhythm and motion began to emerge, but in a context of discontinuity: part of the group self was waking up, while another part was still sleeping or dead (or almost dead), and yet another was silently contemplating the scene. The atmosphere of the room became warmer and more breathable, but feelings of hopelessness, depression and distrust soon made their appearance. Another patient, Jean-Pierre, whose family was of Polish origin, took fright; it was too warm for him, too soon to wake up, and although the atmosphere was now more alive, it was causing some uneasiness. He started to sing in a language which no one understood.

A woman in the group, aged about 50 – Ms Robin – looked at the rest of us as if she were a spectator in a theatre trying to connect the group together with her eyes (or perhaps paralyse them with a hypnotic gaze). In an attempt to understand what was going on, she said: 'I am looking for a place to stay. Nobody invites me. All my children are married but they have no room for me.' I understood her to mean that she was looking for an invitation from the others so as to open up a place for herself in someone else's space. Her own body was not a 'good' home, a place to live in, but a grave – the dilemma of *soma-sema*. *Soma* refers to the body, while *sema* is a tomb. According to Babylonian and Pythagorean philosophy, the soul leaves the body after death and looks for another place where it can stay. Implied in this concept is the transmigration of souls (metempsychosis). Ms Robin personified the group's dilemma – it wanted to come out into the world and live life, but it could not stand being in the open. The group needed to annihilate the gap between its Ice Age and genuine living – it had to find another body which it could inhabit.

After a long silence one patient lit a cigarette; someone else followed suit, and the room soon became 'inhabited' by smoke. This smoke stood for their evanescent but constantly renewed anxiety taking over the whole group-space. In the absence of words, the smoke began to invade the group and take possession of the group mind; it was also an attempt to force the analyst to leave (I do not smoke and am uncomfortable with the practice). I suggested that we try to understand the meaning of this smoke-invaded world.

Our next meeting (we met once a week) was in a bigger room on the ground floor. The patients did not stop smoking but the larger space made the atmosphere more tolerable; they were telling me that, for the moment at least, what I was offering them was no more substantial than smoke. The atmosphere of a group and its 'texture' or 'matter' – solid, liquid or gaseous – is part of a dramatized language which illustrates the kind of 'cement' which holds us together – or not, as the case may be, that is, the group may dissolve and become shapeless.

Looking at the smoke rising, Brigitte, a young patient, imagined a wonderful cathedral. She said: 'This place is beautiful. It's a magnificent church. I am sure that we're going to find help here.' This was her way of expressing the wish to construct a fantasy place; Dominique added her voice to that of Brigitte, saying: 'We should listen to the doctors; they're trying to help.' The depressive heaviness of the group was becoming lighter – the ungainly penguin was being transformed into a cathedral in the sky. This, of course was also a kind of idealization, a means of flight – escaping vertically from an unbearable horizontal existence towards a new dimension (or perhaps an a-dimensional world, one without any dimension at all). Levitation, which opposes gravity, is a way of reacting against life experienced as a catastrophic fall. Heidegger (1927) speaks of falling into the world as constituting the basic ontological experience of life. Existing means being out in the world; in order to exist we need a mother-world to hold us (echoing the mother who contains the child *in utero*).

## The group body comes alive

One month later, the group was more alive but at the same time more distressed. We could see the group experience as a sort of Tower of Babel, a confusing 'theological' meeting-place of different languages with many things taking place at the same time. As the group became more alive – more lively too – it was also more discordant and noisy. Some of the patients wanted to talk, others to sing or dance, to show themselves in as attractive a light as possible, or to let themselves be attracted to some other member of the group. Eroticization at all levels was in open competition with affection and understanding. To oppose integration, the psychotic part of the group was trying to impose discontinuity, disintegration and fragmentation. Fragmentation is the result of a psychotic attack on the group self, the outcome being a psychotic self/group-*persona*.

Brigitte, the 'cathedral' patient, stopped idealizing the situation, became depressed and locked herself into a silent existence. She wanted to leave the hospital, but was unable to. Her plan received no support from her family. Annie-igloo became more alive, opened her Eskimo house and tried very hard to communicate, but the world outside her frozen space seemed to her to be dangerous. She felt that people wanted to steal everything she had: her father stole all her money, she said. Perhaps, for her, giving something (by expressing herself, for example) implied a risk – that her ideas and feelings would be stolen. It must be remembered that the delusional world constitutes a kind of capital investment which patients usually do not want to lose.

One patient mentioned 'Hitler' – a powerful and important figure. Some of the others reacted against the mention of his name, but Dominique said: 'Hitler is inside each one of us'. I understood the group to be going from one extreme to the other, from expansive idealization to destructive narcissism, taking pleasure in destroying and occupying other people's territory. Brigitte began to sing in a sad, monotonous tone of voice. Other patients gesticulated in a stereo-typed kind of way. One patient, Gerard, pronounced the word 'masturbation', whereupon everybody became frantic and uneasy; the whole space was taken over by compulsive masturbation as in Peter Brook's production of Peter Weiss's *Marat/Sade*. Then suddenly the group fell silent and became as mechanical as a lifeless puppet – perhaps an ungainly melancholic penguin. Someone said: 'It's cold in here. We need more heat.'

The group was a multiplicity of things and of beings, shifting from extreme coldness to a need for warmth; masturbation was a burning impulse aiming to stimulate a corpse, a dead body without a future.

## Emotional turbulence

'Life', said Claude-penguin, showing the scars on his body (his mother had had a forceps delivery), 'has left its mark on me from the very beginning, from birth in fact. Destiny is stronger than chance. Everything is marked and measured from the outset.' Showing us his scars was Claude's way of taking on the role of spokesperson for the wounds which the other group members had had to suffer at some point or other in their life. Brigitte, who used to work in a shoe-shop, looked at the medical director of the unit and said: 'You have big feet. You must take size 11.' In other words, she needed to know where the medical director 'stood', and whether he was strong enough to carry such a heavy load, to manage such a weighty (important) function.

Olivier, a young schizophrenic drug addict, spoke about his breakdown: 'I was in the toilet reading a comic strip with the door open and people asked the police to take me away.' A comic strip consists of a series of separate drawings, none of which is capable in itself of 'movement', as is the case with a cartoon film. Olivier's narrative became an image of the group at that moment: different scenes from different eras juxtaposed together, incoherent reality being the result. The picture I had in my mind was that of a puppet with bizarre gestures.

Another patient spoke about his body being as big as the Eiffel Tower. The Eiffel Tower is shaped something like a shoe, vertical and metallic – at any rate greater than the horizontal power of the medical director. To be a metallic construction like the Eiffel Tower is a delusional concept of power – one that is without feelings.

Mr Camus, a member of the group who seldom spoke, said: 'I am not Camus the writer, I'm someone else and I'd like to say a word or two.' 'What do you think of this atmosphere?' I asked, and he answered in a 'psychoanalytic' tone of voice: 'There are three atmospheres here: one of sex and excitement; one of sadness; and another of trying to find a way out.' This patient resembled a prophet – he had a long beard, and he gave the impression of knowing the way forward.

## A life-giving apocalypse

Another patient, Mr Kader, who had recently arrived from Madagascar, realized that the group had already been 'born' before his arrival. Suddenly he began to dance, a frenzied dance which became for some of the group a sort of initiation rite. Olivier stood up and took Mr Kader in his arms. They kissed. At that moment Josette, who was usually Olivier's close friend, became upset and jealous and ran away. 'I don't care about her,' said Olivier. 'She is too crazy. I believe in God; my God is hashish.' (As I mentioned, he was schizophrenic and a drug addict.)

Through affinity, confrontation and competition, the group expressed its different views and beliefs. Annie-igloo spoke about Goethe's *Elective Affinities* (1809), saying that empathy and affinity were important. Mr Kader wanted to become part of the group and to find affinity through Olivier, but Olivier reacted negatively. Delusional personal beliefs do not go well with affinity. 'I am God,' said Olivier, and another group member, Mr Colombo, replied: 'God is dead.' 'I don't believe in my father,' said Olivier. 'My god is myself, when I take hashish.' Hashish was the god which the group used against Aesculapius, the Roman god of medicine; in the group context, it was the god which the child used against the father, the psychoanalyst father-figure.

As we see here, the psychotic experience was taking possession of the transference and counter-transference, and trying to take possession of other people's minds and feelings. But nobody is entirely psychotic; the self is neither completely psychotic, nor wholly neurotic. The psychotic self is a metaphor we use in speaking about the kaleidoscopic experience of chaos and fragmentation which opposes integration. The study of the self in this complex context of a group of chronic psychotic patients brings us to the myth of origins. The primary structure of the ego, wrote Glover (1968), could be figured as a kind of skeletal system which starts off as a cluster of ego nuclei. These 'archaeological' fragments of a primitive ego come back to life in the shape of an unintegrated self which is unprepared for integration. Disintegration involves the chaotic forces of the primitive ego which cannot bear to be born again and emerge from its frozen world. Though certainly a solution to a painful catastrophic experience, it is a drastic one.

Tension between war and peace, between Thanatos and Eros, played a major role at the beginning and end of almost every session; it had a kind of ritual function. Disorder, 'ordinary' order and delusional order were all present. The members of the group tried to speak and to take over the microphone at the same time, as in Bosch's *Ship of Fools* (c. 1490–1500) (Figure 2). In that painting, several people are gathered round something hanging from the tree – an apple? a stone? – in a setting which could be seen as the forerunner of a recording session of some radio programme or other; a preconception, as Bion said, of something which had not yet been invented but nevertheless was already there. The protagonists seem to be talking or singing into a microphone. The space of madness stands in this case for a multiplicity of voices and faces wanting to talk at the same time. A kind of tension emerges before a certain harmony in the painting can be seen and appreciated. Harmony implies a certain order of 'sounds', 'colours' and 'forms', agreement as opposed to disagreement, calm as opposed to emotional turbulence (Bion 1977). A psychotic breakdown is a disturbingly turbulent experience in which birth is inseparable from death, a situation in which the unconscious speaks through a microphone/loudspeaker without repression. However, at a particular moment, repression returns as a necessary rule of law to create meaning out of chaotic nonsense. In 'Emotional

Figure 2 © Photo RMN. Jerome Bosch (1450–1516), *La nef des fous* (Ship of fools)

Turbulence', Bion (1977) speaks of the expectation of the group being so intense that it can hardly wait to hear what is going to be said. This expectation stimulates a great many feelings which may become so powerful that the group becomes resistant to any emotion and falls silent. Silence can be used as a way of creating boundaries in order to shut out a chaotic and uncontrollable experience.

## After the storm

Once the crisis was over, the group suddenly became afraid of its own destructive aggressiveness. That brought order and a feeling of calm in which each participant observed the others, in the expectation of a new climate, one of peace and reconciliation. Jean-Pierre, the patient whose family came from Poland, said: 'We need to be warm with one another'; Annie-igloo, now less 'refrigerated', said that they needed love. Gerard stopped looking at his watch all the time – his delusional messianic timepiece – and looked at me with a warm and lively look in his eyes.

Gradually the atmosphere became more breathable for all of us. Our *Ship of Fools* was navigating in less turbulent waters – perhaps on the lookout for some safe haven or other. Brigitte was both frightened and pleased that the group had started to think and to exist; she realized that it could also break up again and become dismembered and dismantled. There seemed to be a double expectation. On the one hand, they were waiting for the advent of a paternal figure, a constructive phallic element, which would help to bring things together and create a spinal cord that would hold the group intact. (In prehistoric times people lived in shelters made from the skeletons of the great mammoths.) The other expectation was the defeat of the father, tantamount to an attack on linking (Bion 1967 [1959]: 193). Then the idea of a maternal figure came to the fore. The group began talking about a temple, a house, a hospitable place where they could bring all the pieces together, a place to be held, to be kept warm and protected. The function of the group-mother or group matrix is to contain the contradictory forces within it and to pacify the conflict with the father, so that the integrative function of a synthesizing group self can come into its own.

For the *logos* to come into existence, the group matrix must be organized and prepared to accept its advent. Mr Colombo said that we should be silent in order to allow the first true word to be spoken. Claude-penguin suggested that those words should be written down rather than spoken. Writing is made to last. After a pause the group became tense again and the unconscious forces within it, envious of the group 'womb' and its fertility, started to attack. The group's 'Hitler' dimension returned and its narcissistic self again expressed its admiration for him. Dominique spoke again of the danger of Hitler being present inside each participant, in case that particular aspect found itself reawakened.

As in the war between Eros and Thanatos, the members of the group became excited sexually. Life and death – indeed all kinds of contradictory feelings – became eroticized. Eroticism in the form of sadistic fantasies brought a homogeneous quality which took over the whole field of experience: thinking and feeling were just as eroticized as the strictly sexual tendencies.

At one point the erotic tension abated, everything became blocked and frozen again. Then the group began to move, emerging from the frost, trying to understand what was happening. Philip, another young psychotic patient, asked me if I understood Chinese – could I understand the language of the unconscious was what he was really asking – the language of madness, according to another member of the group. Mr Colombo said: 'I am Thanatos, and even Freud can't do anything about that.' Other members of the group started to complain that the Nazis were taking possession of the entire place, attacking harmony and good feelings. Mr Colombo changed his attitude and remembered that he was Jewish. He took off his glasses and looked at them upside-down, saying: 'I am also the other way around, I am anti-Nazi.' He spoke about the *Luftwaffe*, repeating the word '*Luft*' – a reference to air, matter which is light and able to levitate. One patient called the group's attention to the sound of an aeroplane outside; suddenly the whole group felt lighter and someone spoke about being transformed into a bird – but a mad bird which was losing its head. Claude spoke about a crocodile living in his stomach. After a pause something like a miracle took place. Claude looked through the window at the sky; in a state of apparent ecstasy, he said: 'The crocodile is flying away.'

The crocodile then turned into a dragon, a winged spirit of Nature, an earth monster forced to come out into the open, a kind of god, something (or somebody) for the group to believe in. The dragon became a god of madness, the idealized version of delusional thinking. The ideology of madness competes with the ideology of sanity, but madness and sanity are parts of the same body, i.e. the group matrix. Which will behead the other? Will madness be cut off, or sanity? Or will both principles be brought together? The group needed a mediator to clarify this for them. There had to be a bridge between the two, a paternal figure, a *pontifex*/builder of bridges who could link up both worlds.

Olivier spoke of a rider on horseback jumping from one side of the river to the other. This was as though to say that he did not need a bridge, he did not need a father, his god hashish was a strong horse with enough power. Mr Camus, the prophet with the long beard, spoke about taking and not taking risks, saying: 'In order to avoid risks, we need to play on both sides.' Mr Kader said that he felt a great struggle going on in his mind as if something were in danger of being blown up. Mr Colombo said: 'Perhaps we should cut off John the Baptist's head before it explodes.' Someone else then mentioned Salomé and Salomon (my name). In other words, part of the group was playing the role of Salomé, seductively trying to convince another member to be a scapegoat. After this interplay of seduction and fascination, tension within the group rose significantly; then Jean-Paul exploded with laughter, and soon the whole group was laughing.

And so an explosion had taken place – but an explosion of laughter. After this cathartic crisis, the group calmed down and relaxed. Where had the madness gone? Where was the dragon and the delusional beliefs?

At one point, Mr Kader looked outside and made a gesture with his hand, as though to dramatize the fact that group was throwing madness out the window. Again someone heard a plane engine and Mr Kader said: 'The plane is going to blow up, some strange birds have got into the engine.'

In the following session, the idea of 'flying' became mixed up with that of 'stealing'.[2] Cutting off John the Baptist/Salomon's head was a way of stealing his secret thoughts, his power. The group was aware of what it was being offered by me, just as I was aware of what I was receiving from them. Gerard, who usually held his head in his hands, looked up – as though he no longer needed his arms to support his thoughts. The group was feeling less threatened.

Mr Colombo spoke about telepathy and flying thoughts. Claude was still thinking of his stomach. He looked at it, and said: 'The crocodile is in here again and knows everything; it says next summer is going to be hot.' The group reacted to this statement as if summer had already arrived – at times the atmosphere would be too warm and everybody felt too hot. The group could not differentiate between having warm feelings and getting hot (sexually excited). Then Claude said: 'You know, a primitive tribe in the Amazon forest, the Jivaros, are head-shrinkers'.

Ms Chamerois – a patient who was about 60 years of age – sometimes thought she was Queen of France and a descendant of Louis XVIII. She was frightened by the emotional turbulence of all these feelings. She said she felt too hot and that we were in danger of losing our strength and becoming dehydrated.

Group analysis is not without its perils, but it is nonetheless a necessary exploration. To analyse feelings, thoughts and beliefs means also to enter a forest – where Jivaros may be lurking – to go into a primitive and wild environment where archaic tendencies and ancient cultures can be woken up. The group mind is a forest, a forest of primary feelings and wild thoughts.

When a group begins really to think as a group and to experience itself as such, any interruption (for example, at the end of a session) becomes painful because it is felt to be an attack on linking, an attack on thinking. Gerard wanted to change living time to mechanical time, that of his wristwatch; a repetitive and circular time endlessly going round and round (with no risk of separation or end). Like the Jivaros, he wanted to shrink and immobilize experience into a controllable and reduced space, something he could keep a watch over; an iron-covered mechanized time as opposed to a flexible and living time. Catatonic patients tend to petrify space and time.

In the next session someone started talking about a fish, someone else about a snake, then someone added 'smoked fish'. The group-animal, once an ungainly bird, had regressed and turned into a fish. The delusional atmosphere, the smoky climate, dried up the group; without fluids/fluidity, no one knew what to do next. At one point Claude spoke about a dream-like vision he had had about a broken piece of glass from a window: 'This is me, Gerard, when I am a piece of broken glass.' I understood him to mean that coming back to life can be experienced as dangerous when one still feels as fragile as a window-pane; opening-up can become equated with breaking.

Ms Robin (the patient who spoke in the earlier session about not having a home of her own and about being neglected by her children) smiled, and said in a cold and detached tone of voice: 'My brother died,' then added, 'My nephew too, actually, in a car accident.' Jean-Pierre retorted: 'That's not true, the bit about the accident.'

The group then expressed fear of going out of doors – 'We might have an accident'. Closing in on oneself is an autistic defence – yet at the same time the group had to open up to the world and take the risk of encountering danger. The group was still alternating between approaching life and hiding away from it. Ms Robin went on: 'I'm far away from here, 2000 kilometres away. I have gone back to the place where I was born.' Thanks to her, the group ego was escaping, running away from the present into a place in space called time, a faraway time – its origins.

In the following session, the atmosphere was very tense; feelings of distress seemed to have permeated the 'group-skin'. Suddenly Annie, the igloo-woman, broke the silence; she said she felt very angry – furious even, because her mother had stolen something from her and then abandoned her. This session was the first after the summer holiday break; her anger was that of the group, furious at having had two months of their therapy time 'stolen' by the father-figure Resnik, who had abandoned them. The group felt frustrated and hungry. The mouth of the group or child cannot put up with the loss of its object/source of goodness (breast-mother). The absent object can become a frightening hole, a black hole of turbulence which swallows and destroys everything.

Mr Kader spoke about the danger of impure feelings attacking pure ones: 'Impurity is what remains after pure feelings have vanished and been dissipated, but God has the key to everything, He could solve the problem.' Gerard, identified with Mr Kader, seemed to be very anxious. The group's feelings of aggressive greed and devouring were what were being referred to as impure feelings. The atmosphere was becoming more and more stifling.

Without air and the freedom to breathe, the *logos* is deprived of oxygen; the group mouth cannot think nor express any articulate words. Their few remaining thoughts – scared at the idea of suffocating – try to escape, flying away like migrating birds searching for a more conducive climate in which to develop. What remains is a terrifying vacuum, a dense and confused climate of emptiness and loneliness.

How can such an atmosphere be encouraged to change? Claude mentioned the number three: 'Two times three is six, and six makes you think of "seismic"'. The group had perhaps experienced an earthquake, after which the ego had to be found again and brought back to safety in the living body with its dimensions of space and time. The same is true of the family: three stands for the nuclear family (father, mother and child-group); they too have to be brought together. 'Six' is 'double-three' – Claude's 'double' is the group.

After a lengthy silence, Claude opened his mouth (he has almost no teeth) and said that he needed to see a dentist. Everybody identified with Claude's mouth; the group seemed to be demanding a good analyst-dentist capable of repairing the 'holes' in the group-mouth. Claude said he wanted to get rid of these cavities in his mouth; at that point someone mentioned Paradise – a necessary image, now that the group was going through hell with the pain they felt in the group-mouth. Ms Robin said her feeling for life was locked up inside her mind and body. 'There is tension', said Kader, 'between Israel and the Arabs; how are we to prevent a destructive war?' Brigitte, the cathedral-patient, had left the hospital several months before but had had to be readmitted because of a relapse; she had remained tense and silent almost from the start of the session. She now broke her silence, and said something about Christ: 'We need Christ'. She paused, then took off her sweater, rolled it into a kind of rag doll shape and held it in her arms like a baby. 'It's the Virgin Mary and the baby Jesus. I want to keep Christ safe in Bethlehem.' Mr Kader seemed to be very moved. Brigitte continued: 'I'm hungry, I feel empty.' The group became anxious and tense again, until Mr Kader said: 'To avoid war, somebody should give each of us a piece of chocolate.'

In the next session, the group's inner tension was still very present: 'The war is still with us!' someone exclaimed. Annie told us that her parents were always fighting. 'They should have divorced long ago,' she said. Ms Chamerois retorted: 'We shouldn't bother about our parents.' She bent down and showed her back-side to the group. Jean-Pierre said: 'It's cold in here, we ought to have more heat.' Claude's legs began twitching anxiously; he tried to stop them by hitting them. Now that he had come back to life, he was afraid in case he might fall back into his former frozen-penguin state of existence – the prehistory of the group, when it was locked in its glacial Ice Age. 'The other day, I was running in circles,' he said, 'I didn't know what else to do.'

At the end of the session, Jean-Pierre spoke of 'heart' and 'love'. A *locus* is needed if shape is to be given to emotions. The world of madness becomes more coherent, the crew of the *Narrenschiff* (*Ship of Fools*) less mad and life on board more harmonious – at last there is a space for love. The group has become more lively – more alive – and the antagonistic forces of love and hate, Eros and Thanatos, can live together. The group now has access to the outside world, its reality-ego (*Real-Ich*) is able to integrate the pleasure and the reality principles. Their former unconscious misunderstandings or delusions have at last been overcome.

According to Money-Kyrle (1978), sensitive, fragile patients, whether they are mentally ill or not, may transform a misunderstood fact or experience into a delusional version of the truth. This poses a challenge to the reality principle. In the course of development, misconceptions come not only from the child (or, in adults, from their infantile ego) but also from the parents (the superego). If they are not resolved, the opposition between child and adult narcissism leads these misconceptions to take on the force of undeniable 'truth'. The delusional person's unshakeable conviction corresponds to a hardening of these positions.

In the psychoanalytic field – individual, group or institutional – these intrapsychic and interpersonal conflicts have to be brought into the transference in order for them to be worked through. In the transference, delusional beliefs will come up against the psychoanalyst's own convictions (professional narcissism, as it were). However, if the inevitable misunderstandings can be accepted as such by both analyst and patient, the encounter between them will be enhanced and become immediately more human. In the theatre, taking one thing for another was a technique in great use in Molière's time, as in the *commedia dell'arte*. Christine, a schizophrenic patient of mine, once sent to me from Venice a carnival mask representing Harlequin with a long nose – reminiscent of physicians during the time of the Black Death. (Venice was highly cathected by the patient and was part of the transference space, since she knew I was in the habit of travelling there.) I was very disturbed when I received it, and immediately thought that Christine must have been in great distress. I was without any news from her thereafter for several weeks, then I learned that she had been admitted to hospital in a unit which saw no merit whatsoever in the psychoanalytic approach.

When she came back into analysis, she told me: 'I was absolutely fine in Venice. When I came back to Paris, I don't know what happened, I went through some sort of acute crisis, as though there was something forcing me to commit suicide.' In the sessions which followed, she associated from the carnival mask to the time of the Black Death in Venice, and she remembered that when Freud made his famous trip to the United States with Jung and Ferenczi, he said that he was bringing them 'the plague'.

As I mentioned in my discussion of narcissistic depression, when psychotic patients wake up from their delusional state and begin to recover, they have a decision to take: either to adapt to reality and give up their delusional beliefs or to reinforce their psychotic mask. In the latter case, there is a state of tension between the psychotic and the non-psychotic aspects of their personality. Christine enabled me to understand that she felt possessed by a destructive ego disguised as a physician, who opposed any idea of recovery – especially if it came via the 'plague' of psychoanalysis.

The carnival mask was, on the conscious level, a thank-you present for the help I had given Christine and, unconsciously, a poisoned gift – it was that mask which brought about Christine's acute breakdown. The split between envy and gratitude was particularly obvious here, though it exists with every patient, psychotic or not. Thereafter, she spoke of Pantalone, Columbine's joyful father – a very different image from that of the diabolic mask of Harlequin (which is also that of the hospital psychiatrist who wanted nothing to do with psychoanalysis). From the therapeutic point of view, conscious and unconscious conflicts and misconceptions have to be clarified, in both patient and psychoanalyst, so that a new series of negotiations can begin. In chronically ill psychotic patients, any material which is not brought out into the open can lead to a state of psychological inflexibility, characterized by the inability to tolerate doubt and uncertainty. Therapy, in the space of the transference, consists in rediscovering or re-creating an atmosphere of reflective and pre-reflective ambiguity which can be tolerated by both participants. From then on, the individual and group ego can be reconstructed and repaired.

The Sainte-Anne group became a living body – a 'heart', as Jean-Pierre put it. That heart was beginning to re-experience emotions, rhythm, systolic and diastolic pulsations. The group became a complex organism with its various chrono-biological rhythms, one which was endeavouring to integrate a more or less harmonious flow of time.

## The end of our travels

The group analysis lasted three years. Begun in the Ice Age, the life of the group gradually thawed out. Throughout that voyage, the space of the group transference enabled my colleagues and me to share the feelings of the participants; we were thus able to live through the group experience of coming back to life. The metaphors I have used in this chapter – *Ship of Fools* and Pantagruel's sea voyage – have, I trust, conveyed something of the dramatic vicissitudes, the shapes and the colours of the adventure we had embarked upon some three years previously.

End-of-the-world fantasies often have – to some degree at least – the idea of the creation of an entirely new world. Chaos, Apocalypse and Revelation are the three leitmotifs which rhythmed the mystical and delusional voyage of the group. Little by little, the *Narrenschiff* became more alive and more coherent, though it was still difficult to detach it from its 'Dwelling of Truth'. Coming back to life is no easy matter; it is difficult to stand back from the delusional construction by which the group expresses its despair. Wakening up to life once again after a long frozen sleep implies the ontological dilemma of a new life which is about to begin. That is why I wanted to illustrate my analytical experience of the universe of madness with an example taken from an institutional context. It is when we come undone, when the ego begins to break up, that the shift from 'un-being' to 'being once more' takes place – coming back to life with all of its meaningfulness. It is in this space in which time begins to thaw out that the long-stay psychotic patient can decide to establish limits which he or she feels acceptable or tolerable or to open up towards life itself – it is, from the point of view of the patient's future mental health, a life-or-death decision.

I have emphasized many times in this chapter the importance of the emotional understanding and containment which is provided by the group and institutional transference. The turning point, when the delusional ideology can be openly challenged in the transference, is an essential moment in this work. Navigating between the life and death drives, thawing out and deflation of the delusion are crucial events; once the delusion is no longer an unshakeable belief, dis-illusion raises the existential question of the possibility of hope. But there is no hope without despair – thanks to the treatment, the old familiar world is coming apart; loss of the delusional world makes for a process of mourning which is painful and sometimes persecutory. A delusional ideology is a system of ideas, a philosophy, which has its own laws and its own logic, no matter how delusional these may be. A successful outcome is a negotiation between contradictory ideologies.

The journey through what I have called the universe of madness unfolded in a dynamic and complex way in which the value system of the patients' ill part and that of their healthy part were constantly trying to set up some kind of dialogue. At times reciprocity was possible, at others this was not the case. Every delusional conviction stands by its own principles before accepting defeat. The work of the transference (*Durcharbeitung*) is arduous but fascinating; but it has to be done if some mediation is to be established between life and death, between two modes of thought, between two manners of being.

# 5

# Glacial times[1]

Emptiness, silence, heat, whiteness, wait, the light goes down,
all grows dark together, ground, wall, vault, bodies, say twenty
seconds, all the greys, the light goes out, all vanished. At the same
time the temperature goes down, to reach its minimum, say
freezing point, at the same instant that the black is reached, which
may seem strange.

Samuel Beckett, Imagination Dead Imagine[2]

The skipper made answer: Be not afraid, my lord; we are on
the confines of the Frozen Sea, on which, about the beginning
of last winter, happened a great and bloody fight between the
Arimaspians and the Nephelibates. Then the words and cries of
men and women, the hacking, slashing, and hewing of battle-axes,
the shocking, knocking, and jolting of armours and harassements
the neighing of horses, and all other martial din and noise, froze
in the air; and now, the rigour of the winter being over, by the
succeeding serenity and warmth of the weather they melt and are
heard.

By jingo, quoth Panurge, the man talks somewhat like. I
believe him. But couldn't we see some of 'em? I think I have
read that, on the edge of the mountain on which Moses received
the Judaic law, the people saw the voices sensibly. Here, here,
said Pantagruel, here are some that are not yet thawed. He then
threw us on the deck whole handfuls of frozen words, which
seemed to us like your rough sugar-plums, of many colours,
like those used in heraldry; some words gules (this means also
jests and merry sayings), some vert, some azure, some black, some
or (this means also fair words); and when we had somewhat
warmed them between our hands, they melted like snow, and
we really heard them, but could not understand them, for it was
a barbarous gibberish.

Rabelais, *Gargantua and Pantagruel*, Book Four, Chapter LVI,
'How among the frozen words Pantagruel found some odd ones'

In order to continue our journey, I will once again require Rabelais's help, as well as that of Samuel Beckett, who guided me through my first book (and earlier travels) *The Delusional Person* (Resnik 1973). Beckett's plays help me to understand the meaning and the importance of a moment in time, a pause, the meaning of silence and emptiness. Thanks to the characters in his plays, silence becomes an infinite memory, just as nothingness often accompanies the feeling of emptiness in psychotic experience. Rabelais's own trajectory through life, as it is presented in his writings, has at times given me inspiration. It was the meeting between Pantagruel and Panurge the philosopher which introduced a philosophical and poetical dimension into Rabelais's texts.

The group I shall describe in the rest of this chapter resembles a great Pantagruel-like 'stomach', *ventriosus* and *omnipotens* like his father Gargantua. The metaphor of the protuberant stomach leads me back to body language and to the bodily aspects of silence, which are always present in Rabelais's writings as they are in Beckett's plays.

In this chapter I develop my thoughts on ontology as well as what I would call the 'visceral' psychopathological aspects of psychotic thinking. The thoughts and language of the psychotic patient are full of metaphors which often reveal an aesthetic experience. Aristotle's *Poetics* has its sources in metaphor and metonymy; often in psychiatry, these can evoke the idea of neologism and plays upon words (as Freud (1905a) called them in his book on jokes).

Here the reader will find elements to which I have already referred in Chapter 4 on 'The Universe of Madness'. The universe of madness appears this time in another shape, with a different landscape – and it involves another cultural setting, Italy. I shall first describe the circumstances in which I launched into my new nautical adventure, another *stultifera navis* (*Ship of Fools*).

In August 1988 I was invited to give a seminar on psychosis for a group of psychologists and psychiatrists working in the Santa Giuliana Mental Hospital in Verona, Italy. The director of the hospital, Professor Ferlini, was particularly interested in my way of working with psychotic patients and especially in the manner in which I made contact with severely ill patients; he himself was well versed in this kind of work and wanted to do something of the kind with me.

He allowed me to choose whatever teaching method I preferred. Due to the fact that I had been working for many years in institutions, with individuals and with groups, I suggested that we should see some patients in consultation together; in this way, we would be able to share the same experiential field. The idea was to see the patients in a special room with a two-way mirror. Professor Ferlini was to be with me as a participant but silent observer and the rest of the medical staff were to be in the adjoining room behind the mirror, as 'invisible' witnesses. (The members of the group, of course, had been informed about the presence of the medical staff 'through the looking glass', as it were.)

Our first meeting became the starting point both for a clinical research project and for a group therapeutic experience which lasted for over three years.

It was a mixed group composed of patients aged between 20 and 35. Most of the members, about ten in all, were diagnosed as suffering from schizophrenia, and another two presented delusional hypochondriasis and hallucinations. It is very difficult for patients such as these to tolerate psychotic anxiety, which appears to them as a kind of constant panic attack. They cannot cope with life and as a result they become blocked and cold, indifferent and apathetic. Perhaps what is most distressing for any human being is to be confronted with someone who is unresponsive and apparently incapable of feeling – like a reified object or a corpse. Devereux (1967) explains that individuals tend to respond with panic whenever they are faced with the lack of reactivity or unresponsiveness of matter. The need to deny this fact and to control their panic pushes individuals to interpret any physical event in an animistic way, and to attribute meanings to such events which they do not in fact have, in order to be able to experience them as 'responses' to their own acts. The danger, as in every psychoanalysis, is that of remaining monolithically silent and unresponsive – or, on the contrary, of giving an immediate interpretation in order to eliminate counter-transference anxiety (as a psychopathological dynamic aspect of transference and counter-transference). What happens to the verbal and non-verbal communication between patient and psychotherapist or psychoanalyst – or, for that matter, in an institution between patients and staff – depends on their capacity for maternal 'reverie' (Bion), their capacity to contain and to deal correctly with anxiety.

A group discussion followed the second session with the hospital staff (without the patients) so that we could exchange our impressions and feelings about this experience as a work-group. For Bion (1961), notions of task and cooperation are very important topics in the mental life of a work-group.

Freud (1921) discussed the relationship between individual and group psychopathology. Extending the concept of the inner world suggested by Freud and later developed by Klein, one can imagine a multiple world of instinctual drives and objects (internal objects) either cohabiting peacefully or in a state of war. According to Bion, 'The individual is a group animal at war, not only with the group, but also with himself for being a group animal and with those aspects of his personality which constitute his "groupishness"' (Bion 1961: 131).

Keeping in mind Rabelais's model and Hieronymus Bosch's extraordinary painting the *Ship of Fools* – which I used in Chapter 4 as a metaphor – we shall now embark on a long journey. I shall start with our first meeting, the beginning of this historical voyage.

In that first session, a young schizophrenic patient called Natasha (her father had named her after Tolstoy's heroine in *War and Peace*) seemed, like the rest of the group, to be incredibly aloof. Her face was very tense, inexpressive and frozen. Beside her was sitting Loredana – a young hebephrenic patient. She found it very difficult to think for herself. She was like a delicate, empty-headed doll, very dependent on what other people were thinking; a fragile porcelain doll which seemed about to fall to pieces. Her expression and her eyes said that she was either confused or distracted.

Next to her was sitting Silvia – a beautiful young woman who seemed very strange: cold and lethargic, she was reminiscent of a Florentine *Madonna* of Renaissance times. Sometimes her apathy changed into an enigmatic *Mona Lisa* smile. Rossana sat next to her; a young woman, who looked much older than her years – she could have been an elderly depressed woman. Sometimes she looked like a witch, angry and sad, especially when she lowered her head and let her hair fall forward, hiding her face. This patient kept three different diaries, which she had been writing for some three years. She felt able to show two of them to the staff (and thus, indirectly, to me). The third diary remained out of reach, like a sort of intimate, sacred temple (an idealized private part of herself). Although she was not usually able to talk in the group, she could experience her feelings and would express them in an indirect way through her behaviour in the clinic and in her writings.

Then there was Sylvano, a very sad young man, who was hardly in touch with himself or with other people – he seemed to be aware only of his legs, or more precisely, of his right leg. His usual attitude was characterized by unrelenting complaints that his leg felt heavy and tired. With a fixed look and a pained expression on his face, he would say: 'My leg is sad and crushed. My legs are weak and can't support my body.' This was his way of displacing from his mind into his leg – from the upper to the lower part of his body – all the suffering which he was unable to integrate mentally. Curiously enough, this young man had worked in a hosiery department before being hospitalized. This hypochondriacal anxiety, which was delusional in nature, was a sign of his *pathos*, as expressed in the pained yet moving grimace he seemed constantly to wear on his face.

The next patient was Marco – a young man of 27 who was obese and severely schizophrenic. His illness had begun when he was 18, around the time when his mother, not yet separated from his father (who later died), had introduced him to her lover. She had asked him to go out for a drive for a few hours so that she could be alone with her lover. It was then that Marco had had a panic attack, accompanied by a mystical delusional and profound regression, for which he had had to be hospitalized. I had previously treated him individually for a few sessions. He would talk in a delusional way about 'his' sun which was sometimes his friend and sometimes his enemy. He would ask me to close the window because he was afraid of the sun's powerful rays. He used to describe his stomach as a cemetery, a Dantesque space where his father and uncle were buried together with terrifying monsters. He saw me as Buffalo Bill, while he identified with Sitting Bull. Marco demanded a space for himself and his starving tribe of the living-dead. He was very attached to his mother in a symbiotic and erotic kind of way, and was extremely jealous of his mother's lover and of his four sisters; the whole family was paralysed by unbearable anxiety. I advised that

UNIVERSITY COLLEGE Library CORK

he be hospitalized again in the Santa Giuliana clinic in order to treat him individually for a while, then in the group.

His voice was like that of a small child during our first group session, when he seemed to be addressing the Virgin Mary. From time to time his voice would take on a paternal tone, which was both persecutory and violent. He used this tone in order to frighten the rest of the group; he projected into the others his infantile incestuous ego, in order to make them obey his own terrifying superego.

Next to him was Alberto – an intelligent, slim young man who was psychologically very fragile and who had manic tendencies. He often spoke about his girlfriend, who had died in a car accident. He, however, was convinced that her death was entirely his fault – he claimed that she had died as a result of a football match in which Verona, his favourite team, had beaten Turin – the one his girlfriend supported.

Lastly there was Maximo. He too was overweight, and was always obstinately silent, cold and detached. Sometimes he would manifest his presence by expressing a need for a space of his own in his parents' flat. He would say: 'At home I don't have a proper room to myself, everything is full.' From this I understood that in his body – no matter how big it was physically – there was no room for him, for his own self. Other things were occupying the space and filling up the emptiness he felt inside. He always had the impression of being shut in, immobilized, paralysed in some little corridor of his body-house; at other times he would feel far away, out of reach of his own self, scattered far and wide over many a long distance. Sometimes he would hug himself, suggesting a sort of symbiotic condensation of mother and child; he seemed to be traumatized in and by his body. He was a kind of imaginary centaur figure, half-mother, half-child.

In the first few minutes of our inaugural session the silence was tense and impenetrable. An impression of defiance, persecution and at times sadness contrasted with the despairing and panicky looks on the faces of these patients who so very much needed help. Initially, all eyes were on me and Professor Ferlini. The patients seemed to be seeking support from us both as a helpful parental couple and as representatives of the institution. We could at times be non-differentiated, like a bicephalous centaur (phallic or 'bi-phallic' mother, a kind of Kleinian monster-figure).

I noticed that Sylvano was looking at his 'bad' leg, and that Rossana, hiding witch-like behind her hair, was looking at her feet. I commented that these two patients were expressing the group's depressive feelings and fear of falling to pieces – a catastrophic depression. In response to their depressive dejection, Alberto proposed that the group should imagine themselves climbing a mountain. He wanted to cheer them 'up', in other words; he used the image of the mountain to suggest seeking help from above. He said that on the top of the mountain there would be a cross or crucifix: his was a mystical approach. For a moment, I imagined Rossana personifying the depressed part of the group flying off into the air on her broomstick. She believed in magic and was convinced that she was responsible for her mother's death, which coincided with her hospitalization: her illness and their separation must have killed her mother, she thought. Between a depressive fall and a manic ascent – despair and hope – the idea of God emerged in the group's unconscious fantasy: the therapist as ideal ego. They were waiting for maternal and paternal help. I felt that through their depressive feelings they were expecting me to be a sort of paternal, divine 'puppet-master' (to use the term employed by one of the group) – a powerful demiurge able to put them back on their feet and support them.

Marco addressed the group, suggesting that they should all participate in some sporting activity or other (overcoming mental pain and suffering by means of action). Somebody mentioned basketball, while Alberto suggested football. After an expectant silence, a change took place in the climate of the group.

With psychotic patients, the content and experience of the transference atmosphere often become passive and inert, as though empty of any life-force (Resnik 1986). It is also the case that in situations of danger one of the reactions of the ego is to try to prevent any motion or 'e-motion' from entering into the experience of daily life. Repressed or denied feelings are coagulated as it were, and transformed into a dense, stifling and polluted atmosphere. When some possibility of change emerges in the group climate, this deadness can be transformed into living matter. Movement appears, with a pulsating, oscillating rhythm – the nature of this movement, of course, may be either constructive or destructive. That is what was happening during this silent, pregnant pause. It was as if Eros and Thanatos as living forces were coming together in a 'substantial' union of forces. Changing from a static model to a dynamic one requires movement – in other words life – in the form of real and substantial energy.

Marco, who looked like a large balloon, personified the group's infantile, greedy and somewhat nonsensical demands. As I pointed out earlier in this book, the term 'folly' derives from the Latin *follis* – a wineskin full of air. A foolish or deluded mind is a sort of wineskin-balloon full of air (the patient's megalomaniac feelings or ideas), which can be either blown up so destructively that it bursts or catastrophically deflated. It may even blow up the whole group. This definition of 'folly' helped me to develop my ideas on narcissistic depression, and on inflation and deflation of the ego ideal in psychosis.

With his chubby inflated face, Marco insisted upon his oral–erotic demands; he tried to impose his will on the group as a personification of the maternal figure he had cathected so intensely. I commented that his favourite inflated balloon was perhaps his mother's breast, to which he was emotionally and sexually fixated. This attachment had become even more symbiotic and erotic when a doctor advised the mother to be more affectionate towards him. Such misunderstandings, in which affection becomes confused with erotic feelings, play a very important role in the pathological development of children and perhaps in the emergence of a psychosis.

At one point Marco looked at a crucifix which was nailed to the wall and spoke once more of the Virgin Mary and the Christ child – a reference to an idealized mythical relationship with his mother. This relationship of course was part of a triad, the third element of which was the missing father; the figure of Joseph the carpenter often seemed to Marco to be the victim in this situation. The Holy Spirit, for Marco, was often identified with his mother's lover, who had pushed Marco's father out of the picture. One day he spoke about a mouth with three teeth: one he called the Virgin Mary, the second the Christ child, and the third Joseph. From time to time he called Joseph 'Peter', the name of his mother's lover. Marco saw the group as an enormous mouth, voracious and incestuous, which was trying to chew and digest the reality of this complicated Oedipal triad.

Rossana, the witch-like, melancholic girl whose long hair covered her face, smoked cigarette after cigarette, a look of utter despair on her face. 'In this place you die,' she said kicking out with her right foot as if aiming a sort of balloon-bomb into the corner of the room where there was a wash-hand basin. Something (a 'folly'-bubble) was about to burst inside the group stomach. A hallucinated voice coming from her stomach was telling her to leave the room before a catastrophe occurred. 'That's my mother's voice,' she said. She listened to what the voice was saying, then left the room. At that point, Alberto stood up, then sat down on the chair Rossana had left vacant. With a cigarette between his lips, he raised his head, the cigarette jutting out into the air; he said, 'I'm putting the voice which says "In this place you die" into my cigarette, I'm going to turn it into smoke and send it up to paradise.'

That was how the group faced up to the conflict between its life and death drives. Accumulated time in a state of 'chronicity' (from *chronos*) was in the process of awakening and being transformed into a time-bomb about to explode. Rossana had done her best to kick the balloon-bomb into the far corner of the room near the wash-hand basin – maybe a firefighter would attend to it and neutralize the risk of an apocalyptic blaze. The other alternative was Alberto's alchemic proposition – incorporating (introjecting) the bomb into his cigarette then projecting it upwards; transformed into smoke, it would vanish. This was a sort of alchemist's sublimation in the service of a magician/witch-mother (the primitive Kleinian mother-figure): Rossana.

Faced with Rossana's individualistic and egocentric decision, spurred on by her dead mother's voice, Alberto took it upon himself to play the charismatic and Messianic role of saving everybody. The mountain expedition became a procession to heaven where there stood a metaphoric and poetic cross anchored in the sky. Confronted with the depressive feeling of being 'down' or falling down to (mother) earth, part of the group reacted with an ascending movement towards the supreme Father.

A tense and stifling silence ensued, full of anxiety but also of life. Alberto, in his role as a shaman-like omnipotent alchemist, went towards the basin in the corner to ascertain whether he had succeeded in transforming the balloon-bomb. He washed his hands and looked at himself in the mirror. Several patients then stood up as though accomplishing a ritual, went towards the mirror and looked at their reflection. Sometimes they looked also at the two-way mirror – perhaps this was their way of identifying with the clinicians by dramatizing their need for an observing ego which would help them gain some insight into themselves and discover their mental space, their inner world.

Alberto drank a glass of water and, with many a dramatic gesture, made a speech about the end of the world and its subsequent rebirth. He seemed to be addressing the whole world, explaining the cataclysms which were about to fall upon our planet; he saw these as a reproduction of the Flood of biblical times. As though he were a prophet, he announced: 'The sky will be torn in two; everything on earth will become cold after the catastrophe.' I understood him to mean a regression to glacial times. Another member of the group claimed that 'an atomic bomb had exploded, but afterwards there would be a resurrection'.

This kind of metaphysical atmosphere in the group echoed a state of anxiety and deep regression in the transference; it represented an escape from and an aesthetic solution to their mental suffering by means of a flight towards the frozen past. The Flood represented a thawing out of the frozen group-world. I use the word 'metaphysical' to express the atmosphere illustrated in some of De Chirico's paintings. 'Meta'-physics means beyond the physical world. The impression in the group was that of an experience which goes beyond ordinary sense-data. Perhaps an appropriate word would be something equivalent to the German term *das Unheimliche*, translated into English as 'The "Uncanny"' (Freud 1919).

In the discussion which followed the session, one of the observers behind the two-way mirror, Dr Flavio Nose, made an interesting point about the difference between maternal and paternal 'reverie'. Bion introduced the concept of maternal reverie, which has to do with containing the nameless dread of the child (here, of the child-group). Paternal reverie has to do with organizing disorder and helping to give it structure in space and time. Both transference functions, maternal and paternal, enable the group's feelings and thoughts to be given back to them in a more tolerable ('digestible') form. With the ability to see life emerging, feelings of persecution and depression come once again to the fore, so that a new form of emotional harmony will have to be discovered.

Marco, the overweight schizophrenic patient, began to speak about how difficult life was – it was all too much for him. His stomach was a problem for him – it was full of prehistoric animals and important people from his past and present life; they were beginning to waken up from a nightmarish hell. He spoke of claws digging into his stomach, Christ's fingernails penetrating into his mind and hurting his stomach. However, this pain was also a symptom of his new-found attachment to life; nails and claws also anchored him to the earth and helped him not to be sucked up into the cosmos (his delusion).

Marco's father had been an animal lover, and he had been especially fond of horses. (Marco imagined the group as a small stable, in which he would be the little pony.) His uncle had been a photographer, and had worked with Fellini, the famous film director. Marco often confused the name of Professor Ferlini with that of Fellini. This phonetic equation conveyed the presence of an admired father and idealized uncle/super-ego figure in the group transference. The image of the father was at times devalued and at others so excessively inflated and idealized that it was transformed into God himself or the cross upon which the Son had been crucified. The group as a global entity took on the role of the mother – sometimes that of the Virgin Mary holding the Messiah (the Christ child) in her arms. A symbolic relationship was established between the crucified Christ (nails on the cross, fingernails) and Marco's stomach. Marco was the embodiment of the group myth and the ritual repetition of a dramatic situation which had turned into delusional thoughts. Marco was equated with the child-Messiah, the fruit of an original sin to which was assigned the task of saving the mother-world and the whole of humankind.

The group's regression to glacial times was its reaction to the possibility of radical change – but one which would be experienced as catastrophic, in Bion's (1970a) words, a turning point involving fundamental change. At such moments, there is a mixture of primitive anxieties and positive emotions which can be revealed in the *hic et nunc* of the transference relationship. In his paper on primary ontological anxiety, Freud (1985 [1915]) discusses the notion of *Real-angst* (anxiety in the face of a real danger). *Real-angst* is an emotional reaction which is generated when individuals are confronted with their own 'Angst' (anguish, anxiety) about unexpected or unknown phenomena. *Real-angst* is manifested when unanticipated incidents overwhelm one's everyday routine. The tendency for delusional thinking to be repetitive and to follow routine is a safeguard against intrusions. A group which has been petrified, frozen or made inanimate will rebel against the feeling of danger entailed in any catastrophic integration back into ordinary life.

In another session, the group gave the impression of mental paralysis – an inability to make associations, to evoke emotions (pleasant or unpleasant) and to accept movement. Only Alberto seemed to be alive – perhaps even a little too euphoric. He looked at the carpet, where he discovered a bit of thread attached to a label which had a goose printed on it. He had therefore found his 'thread of thought'. 'Geese have no soul, they are unintelligent and stupid,' he said. In saying this he defined himself as leader of the group, the other members of which were goose-like, stupid, unable to think or to make associations. Silvia, the Renaissance beauty, smiled enigmatically – confirming how important it was that the living thread of the group had been found again. The danger, of course, was that they might lose the thread of what they had been saying. Silvia, then, was the first to 'attach' herself to this thread of speech; with feeling, she spoke of her inner world. 'I have a great emptiness inside me, a memory blank . . . I can't remember things and that makes me angry with myself.' The associations which she made seemed to confirm the despair and rage she felt – sometimes at her illness, at other times at life in general or at any help which was being offered her. She went on: 'The thread could also be a rope to hang yourself with.'

At that moment, Rossana (the patient who had kicked the bomb away) seemed to react to Silvia's statement about the rope. I commented: 'The voice who said "In this place you die", is posing a challenge to life, transforming the thread of rediscovered thoughts into a rope of death.'

This interplay of contrasts – the war between the life and death drives – created a state of crisis in the group.

It is interesting to look at the etymology of the word 'thought' in correlation with the idea of thread. It was the thread of the spinners in ancient times which first defined the act of thought. *Pensée* (the French word for thought) comes from *pensum*, the quantity of wool which spinners had to spin each day for the production of cloth. That was their daily task – *pensum facere*. Hence the expression 'thread of thoughts' (compare the thread of an argument). Much the same line of thought can be found in the English verb 'to ponder', initially meaning to weigh, and later developing into the notion of thinking.

Once the lost thread had been rediscovered, the empty and useless group mind could change from being a stupid goose into a living network of intelligent communication. The members of the group became spinners and were able once again to think. With my help and that of the healthy parts of the group ego, they were able to continue spinning their 'pensum' for that day in the context of our institutional life as a work-group.

Thread is an important concept in such a group, because it is a nexus between one thought and another – an articulated bridge, the spinal cord of the mental apparatus, which is able to tolerate feelings and thoughts, link them together and give them shape and meaning. The psychological spinal cord stands for the introjected phallic function of the institution-as-father, with its capacity for reparation and restoration. Its mission is to 'vertebrate' the maternal containing function of the individual mind, of the group mind, or of the institution as a whole so as to be able to create order and coherence.

When a frozen river begins to thaw, the fantasy of a biblical Flood emerges. This corresponds also to an apocalyptic sense of 'psychic bleeding', with its attendant danger of a haemorrhage – hence the need to know the clotting or coagulation time of the group's 'life-blood', as a patient once pointed out to me. This is when a 'catastrophic change' may come about.

Becoming aware of the importance of such phenomena is a turning point for the group – a critical moment, in fact. 'Crisis' is derived from the Greek, *krino*, which implies the idea of separation or differentiation; more generally, it can mean a difficult judgement on a critical issue which may lead to a decisive transformation. My long experience with psychotic and non-psychotic patients has confirmed my hypothesis that, for better or for worse, a crisis is always a decisive moment of lucidity (Resnik 1985b).

When a group considers itself to be 'as stupid as a goose' and then begins to be able to think again, some suffering inevitably arises. Being intelligent indicates that they have found their 'head' again, the thread of what they were saying and feeling. Alberto, after having found the thread in the group's magic carpet, examined the label and commented that the drawing of the goose 'looks like a map of Poland – the country bordering on Russia'. The free associations of the group with my name – Resnik, which was probably Russian or Polish for them, connected me with that country. They felt the need to place me in the geography of their history. What was my 'label'? And did I have a magic carpet to help them on their way?

Bion wrote of the Messiah (or mystic image personified by a little god) as being the ideal charismatic child, to whom the holy couple give birth in a pairing group (Bion 1961). The charismatic child, like Christ, personifies the hope and the beliefs of the group. Producing a Messiah (a person, an idea or a utopia) corresponds to the need to give shape to the ideal ego of the group self. In his article 'The Mystic and the Group', Bion (1970b) examines the Messiah fantasy in terms of the mystic and charismatic ideal of the group. The danger – which is also a necessity – is the dis–illusion or deflation of the idealized image; if this occurs creatively, the patients will be back in touch with their true system of non–delusional values.

While this was going on, the group of observers who had been on the other side of the mirror discussed the importance of sensations and feelings. When a psychotic patient seems paralysed or frozen emotionally, what attitude should one take? How does one feel when this occurs? Aspects of the institutional transference between the patient and members of staff were debated. What is the emotional attitude of the psychiatrist, psychologist or nurse who feels emotionally involved in the therapeutic process? One staff member remarked, 'Yesterday, watching the group, I felt confused; I couldn't understand what was happening; I had the impression that the patients were saying something important, but in an inarticulate and apparently disjointed way.' Another psychiatrist spoke of the depressive feeling of the group, which had particularly moved him. Another mentioned the anxiety and fear that the group members had of everything that came from outside, including the other patients and myself. They were impressed, however, by the general 'versatility' of the group and by its ability to represent in such a subtle way some deeply disturbing experiences.

They observed that the group climate had been glacial until Rossana expressed her hostility and left the room. At that point, the group became very excited. The group temperature suddenly shot up, as though in an atomic fallout. The group ego seemed to be bursting out of its paralysis. Some staff members were sensitive to the persecutory aspects, while others were more in contact with the relaxed and serene atmosphere which reigned from time to time.

These sudden climatic variations in the patient group seemed to me to be a succession of Ice Ages, with interglacial periods of relief. I imagined these periods of relief as cracks in the ice, through which some emotional heat could break through. An intensely regressive state appeared from time to time in the history of the group and was manifested in the transference as a real affect.

Another member of the team had noted that a merciless battle of contrasting emotions had been taking place in the session. I suggested that it derived from the struggle between the life and death drives, or perhaps from the ongoing tension between split-off psychical agencies.

Marco manifested the group's tendency towards splitting in the way he changed his voice, which was sometimes depressive in tone and at others thundering – especially when he identified with a paternal superego which was both critical and tyrannical.

After Rossana had felt the need to leave the group in such an aggressive way, her psychiatrist, who was one of the observers, went into the corridor to ask her what was wrong. She replied, 'My father and my mother are dead; and these two dead people are in the process of waking up . . .'.

Waking up from an Ice Age implies coming back to life, and Rossana's relationship with her internalized dead parents meant that she was getting back in touch with that part of her own ego which had died with them. Klein (1940) pointed out that it is not so much the object which is lost but the relationship with that object – in other words, a part of the subject's own ego is inevitably involved whenever we speak of object loss. Rossana was at that moment the spokesperson for the feelings of mourning which the group could not otherwise express. In 'Mourning and Melancholia', Freud (1917 [1915]) writes of the shadow of the (lost) object falling on the ego; I think that the shadow of the group subject, capable of integrating emotionality and experiencing grief, also falls on the ego.

Another colleague remarked that Natasha, who was usually devoid of feelings, had a sad, emotional expression on her face when Rossana returned. It was as though painful emotions and distressing reality had come back into the room with Rossana and had been introjected by Natasha. It seemed to me that Rossana's momentary absence had been experienced by the rest of the group as an opportunity for them to liberate themselves from intolerable fantasies. The group ego was too fragile to tolerate any exhumation of primal loss. Rossana represented Charon in the underworld of Hades, though here she had to ferry the shadow of the dead back to life. Terrified by this, she fled the room. In encouraging her to go back to the group, her psychiatrist had therefore acted like an auxiliary ego.

Griesinger's (1882) 'basic depression' re-emerges in the transference as the return of the repressed. Reintrojection into the current group space of something which happened earlier (the time when repression took place) comes back as a fantasy which is both persecutory and moving. In the history of every psychosis, the ego has been subjected to the traumatic loss of an object relation; the ego feels 'broken' and dispersed. Old wounds are again opened up, and the group is upset and anxious.

Rossana's task in her role as Charon was to transfer the lifeless aspects of the group members, their internal ghosts, down the river of the Lower World. Now the dormant object relations in Hades were waking up; the group body was becoming a living body, though the price to pay was pain and suffering.

The group's life and death drives were in turn dominant, and the sheer warmth of their feelings threatened to set them ablaze – the contrast was too great with their cold and frozen sensations. That posed the problem of a catastrophic phase of thawing out and the fear of a flood. The group ego was ambivalent – it was an era of interglaciation.

On the other hand, feelings of grief and mourning (Rossana's dead mother) appeared symbolically in the form of a shadow of the living-dead. Rossana had indicated to a nurse her fear that if she stopped hallucinating, her mother's voice would disappear forever. The hallucinations were one way for Rossana to keep her internal cemetery alive and still talking; this would help to fill the emptiness of intolerable or persecutory absences.

In the paper I have just mentioned, Freud (1917 [1915]) discussed psychosis and the related problem of depressive emptiness. The returning shadow of the absent object often takes on the appearance of a ghost or a vampire which sucks the life-blood of the group. This reminds me of the shadow of Nosferatus projected onto a wall in Murnau's film *Nosferatu* (Resnik 1993).

In the discussion seminar, Rossana's doctor told us that after the first session, Rossana had gone to visit her brothers and sisters in Bolzano. In addition, she consulted the psychiatrist who had referred her to the clinic in Verona. Rossana told him that she was afraid of getting better, if it meant that the 'ghosts' she used to have inside her were going to return. She did not want to take on the responsibility for what happened to her in life. Our colleague in Bolzano told us of this, and I pointed out later in the group that this was an example of indirect communication: Rossana, like all psychotic patients, needed to proceed in that manner in order to express certain experiences which she would have found intolerable to communicate directly.

In my book, *The Delusional Person* (Resnik 1973), I develop this idea of the 'phobia of proximity' common to psychotic patients and their need to communicate at a distance through transitional spaces, elements, objects or people such as doctors, nurses or other patients. The Bolzano psychiatrist, in Rossana's case, was acting as her spokesperson, and he communicated to us something which would not have been otherwise transmitted.

The patients in the group knew that we were being observed through the mirror by the staff. This too was a kind of transitional phenomenon; it served as a means of communication through a wall which was both transparent and opaque. The psychotic patient's direct and indirect modes of communication can be identified in the behaviour of the institution as a whole. The patient's fragile ego may find it difficult to accept any direct form of interpretation – such an approach could be experienced as an intrusion into the patient's personal world. Taking the necessary care implies an assessment of the optimum distance from which we can talk to the patient with some hope of being understood. I think that there is always an optimum point which, in optics, is called the focal point (of a crystal, for example). Respecting the necessary distance with sensitivity will help to avoid shattering the fragile ego of the patient. Freud (1933 [1932]: 59) compares the psychotic ego to a crystal. He writes:

> If we throw a crystal to the floor, it breaks; but not into haphazard pieces. It comes apart along its lines of cleavage into fragments whose boundaries, though they were invisible, were predetermined by the crystal's structure. Mental patients are split and broken structures of this same kind.

Then he adds, speaking about these patients:

> They have turned away from external reality, but for that very reason they know more about internal, psychical reality and can reveal a number of things to us which would otherwise be inaccessible to us.

Rossana, as the mythical spokesperson for the most regressive part of the group, personified the fixation point from which the ego turns away when faced with a traumatic situation in the present. The concept of 'dispositional points' was developed by Freud in *Three Essays on the Theory of Sexuality* (1905b) as well as in his study of Senatspräsident Schreber (Freud 1911). As he was writing the *Three Essays*, Freud was already concerned with the innate variety of sexual constitutions and the concept of regression. Freud uses the concept of the point of fixation – the point to which the regressive phenomenon may be traced back – as well as the concept of the choice of neurosis, which he had suggested in 'The Neuro-Psychoses of Defence' (1894) and later developed in his papers on the aetiology of neurosis (1898, 1906).

In the case of Rossana, the fact that her hospitalization had coincided with the illness and sudden death of her mother increased her magical belief in the traumatic situation and in her own (presumed) responsibility. Given her egocentricity, she felt that she was the primary cause of her mother's life and subsequent death.

One could add, from a Kleinian standpoint, that censorship corresponds to a primitive and extremely persecutory superego. For Klein, the death instinct corresponds to one of the first persecutory figures.

In the transference experience the psychoanalyst is both a witness to and responsible for the fact that certain patients cannot tolerate their own basic ontological solitude. The patient's phobic and greedy aspects endeavour to take over people and spaces in the environment. This form of expansion of the ego is not the same thing as massive projective identification. It is a more primitive process which aims to 'occupy' any surrounding space which may be experienced as potentially threatening.

For psychotic patients, the world is a mixture of anxiety and panic. Sylvano, the young man who complained of his leg, was very often in a state of panic. He would say to his leg: 'You're afraid, you're panicking'.

The group space was shrinking and was represented somatically by Sylvano's leg. A hypochondriacal phenomenon of this nature often occurs when new patients enter the group, in this case Ornella, Sandra, Ludovico, Christian, Alice and others.

Ornella personified the classically difficult borderline patient whom Malcolm Pines (1978) describes in his article 'Group Analytic Psychotherapy of the Borderline Patient'. She used to be a primary-school teacher; being very narcissistic, she tended to experience the group – and, indeed, the whole clinic – as if we were her 'children', that is, her pupils. In this way she was able to split off her regressive, infantile and devalued self and project it into other people. She was thus able to retain her omnipotent ego ideal; she attempted also to personify the ideal ego for the other patients, so as to be able to control and to manipulate any 'fragments of reality' which she could not accept as being part of herself. When she was not able to control these fragments, she would become aggressive and violent. When these fragments were projected on to the staff, she could blame the staff for anything untoward that happened to her. Treating them disdainfully was part of her destructive, demanding and critical personality. There were days when she felt better and quieter; but these periods did not last long. She was so narcissistic that she could not express any gratitude towards the staff. Being helped always implied for her a narcissistic wound, and this provoked in her a demand for revenge. She became very attached to Loredana, the inexpressive, hebephrenic patient I mentioned earlier.

In one session, Loredana looked out of the window and said, 'How nice the garden is! And the birds are singing so beautifully!' After a pause she said, 'I'd like to leave the clinic. I'd like to walk through the garden, stop a car in the street, and ask them to take me home. I like hitch-hiking.' In Italian, hitch-hiking is called *auto-stop*, which personified her pathological idea as regards experiencing time: stopping life automatically. Another way of doing this, of course, would be to commit suicide. As she looked out of the window, she evoked a fantasy of throwing herself into a river. I learned in the post-session discussion that both Loredana and Ornella had attempted suicide several times. The two women became very close, forming a kind of suicidal couple.

As the group would often speak about Christ and the crucifixion, I understood that they were associating Ornella's attacks against linking with the idea of crucifixion – the supreme sacrifice. These attacks stood also for a murderous, envious attack against the paternal function represented by the director of the clinic, and against the maternal function personified by the institution as a whole.

At the end of the first year, Sylvano, the young hypochondriacal man who suffered 'only' because of his legs, spoke of an important change which had taken place within him. He said: 'Yesterday evening my legs were OK, but my ego had a bad attack of diarrhoea. Today my hands are sweating profusely, I don't know why. Is water leaking from my intestines and out through my hands?' While he was speaking, Giovanni, who was sitting next to him, looked sadly from me to Sylvano. The atmosphere was depressive, and the group was experiencing itself as a huge leg which was weary and sad. Sylvano's leg, the symbol of the group feeling, represented the inability of the group body-ego, tired and fragile, to stand the strain. Now that the group self had been touched emotionally, it began to thaw out and to express itself in a depressive manner – by 'crying', shedding tears through the medium of Sylvano's intestines and hands.

I gave that interpretation to the group. The sadness which accompanied their search for a pair of welcoming maternal arms and for the organizing strength of a father was also a means of protection. It allowed them to express their depressive and paranoid anxiety, helped them become integrated and satisfied their needs. As I watched Giovanni's and Sylvano's eyes become sadder, I commented that the group as a whole was crying through their hands and intestines because of their inability to shed tears through their own eyes. Suddenly Giovanni, as Sylvano's *Doppelgänger* (the double of the self) or shadow, started crying. The thawing of the glacial times was transformed by the group into tears; a situation which expressed the capacity of the group self to get back in touch with its body-ego.

Sylvano had deposited in his leg his 'mourning and melancholia', and he invited the rest of the group to do likewise: the narcissistic satisfaction of the scapegoat. His leg symbolized the group's hypochondriacal mechanism or process of dissociation, which gradually moved upwards from his leg to the intestines, then to his 'sad and weeping' hands, and finally to his head. Here the mental pain which had previously been pushed aside could finally be experienced. Giovanni represented the ability to think about and to mourn the loss of the object. The part of the ego which remained 'attached' to the object follows it, implying therefore the loss of part of the ego. This wound in the 'mental body' is accompanied by distressing feelings of loss.

In the normal mourning process, according to Klein (1940), the individual is able to experience pain and suffering but tries also to bring back the memory of the loved object – 'to reinstate the lost loved object in the ego' (Klein 1975 [1940]: 353). In pathological mourning, the individual feels incapable of safeguarding the good aspects of the lost object so as to be able to reintegrate them inside. Instead of the object, there is a gaping wound. With the passing of time, unbearable feelings of loss are replaced by a lack of emotionality – emptiness and apathy paralyse the affects. This is what was taking place in this group of young chronically ill patients.

Delusional thinking is a characteristic feature of the psychopathology of psychotic patients. The term delusion (*Wahn* in German) designs a complex of thoughts more or less organized (*Wahnideen*) which do not belong to the ordinary way of thinking about everyday reality and its experience. It leaves the 'furrow' normally traced by thinking, and forms a system based on a series of unshakeable convictions – delusional ones – which try to impose their manner of being on the patient's environment.

A delusion is a pathological solution but a 'necessary' one when none better can be found. A delusion is a pathological illusion; dis–illusion, the dissolution of the delusional megalomanic world, represents a new catastrophic experience. Idealization of the lost object (or of the persecutory one) is under threat; danger comes also from the fact that the delusional principle will have to face the reality principle. The reality principle, of course, maintains that delusional thinking is a kind of mystification. This leads to a narcissistic dis–illusion which can be extremely painful for the ego – the need to accept the fact that one has been mistaken all along. Delusional thinking entails loss of the ego ideal and this is an intolerable narcissistic disappointment. Narcissistic beliefs go through a crisis, yet the patient needs his or her delusion.

In our group of psychotic patients, as they became more and more aware of their delusions there was also the feeling of great loss. Narcissistic depression implies the loss not only of an idealized object (or even one looked upon as sacred) but also of the most precious part of the personality. The deflation of the delusion implies loss of the patient's economic and sometimes even cultural capital (compare Freud's (1911) case-study of Senatspräsident Schreber).

Egocentric delusional states of mind transform and distort the nature of the value system of the surrounding culture. The deluded ego endeavours to impose its 'religious' views and to convert any other belief which questions its own convictions. The psychotic part believes that everyone else should modify his or her views and be shaped by the delusional conception. Professor Ferlini and I experienced the sensation of being swallowed up by the enormous mouth of the group, a gaping abyss, a black hole. On the other side of the mirror, the observers too felt as though they were going to be swallowed up by this wide-open yawning gap.

Marco's delusional relationship with the group–mother was often expressed in the group transference as a strange mixture of desperate and erotic sensations. There seemed to be a confused and disturbing concoction of substances and states of matter (solid, liquid or gas), which ended up taking over the whole space and time of the session. There was often an impression of deep states of regression in the transference, as if observing the birth of language and the beginnings of thought. The climate of the session was conveyed by a nebulous atmosphere; sometimes one of the patients would start to cry. Thereafter, nothing could stop the flow of tears. It was like a thunderstorm; once it was over, there would be a state of primary anxiety which up till then had been repressed into the group-body – or, via projective identification, 'repressed' somewhere outside (towards another patient, for example). This all re-emerged in the transference, usually in a painful and distressing way. The Latin word *dolus* implies the idea of being in the kind of pain which is normally closely linked to the mourning process. Memory traces relating to the ego's primitive biography re-emerge, which the body is unable to contain or re-create.

In one session, Sandra, a patient who had recently joined the group, created a tense climate which the observers in particular noticed. She began by describing herself as suffering from what I thought she called a '*heterotopic delusion*' – I thought she had an unusual or different ('hetero-') theme ('topic') in her delusion. When I asked her what this meant for her, she replied: 'When my head is aching badly I need to plunge my brain into a recipient full of ether. That's why my delusion is *ethero*-topic.' One of the characteristics of schizo-phrenic thinking is the phenomenon called phonetic equivalence, which is part of the proto-symbolic process. (See my remarks on this point p. 45.) Shortly afterwards, Sandra felt 'deflated'; deprived of her delusional ether, she was at the mercy of her internal persecutors and of her overwhelmingly depressive feelings. This intolerable suffering made her panic, and she hallucinated a monster on the ceiling of the room we were in. This monster was a chimera – a spider-mother or primitive Medusa-like figure with a dog's head. As we listened to Sandra, her gestures and facial expression terrified and fascinated us. She petrified the group, which became anxious and almost went into a hallucinatory state. Sandra-Medusa knew she was mortal, as in the myth. The group played the part of Perseus' shield – the mirror in which she saw her own reflection and knew that she was mortal. That is when the phenomenon of narcissistic depression or deflation of the delusional ideal ego appears – when the patient discovers his or her own flattened image in the mirror. The ensuing feeling of frustration can be very intense indeed.

In the seminar discussion after this session, we talked about the danger of being disillusioned by oneself. Professor Ferlini mentioned during the seminar that Sandra had spoken to him of the hallucinated monster (the chimera with a dog's head), which she had projected on to the ceiling of the room. She associated to an empty packet of cigarettes which her father had twisted out of shape and had made into that of a monster. Thereupon, he threw the empty packet away. In this way, the containing packet-mother had turned into a terrifying primitive spider-mother. This frightening object had been thrown up on to the ceiling (evacuative projection); it then became a 'bizarre object', a dangerous chimera. Some obscure fear rose in her as she lost hold of her 'ethero-topic' delusion. She could no longer anaesthetize her feelings; her delusional solution no longer worked. She was at the mercy of the pain which her old wounds, henceforth reopened, were inflicting on her.

For Sandra, the group seemed to have become an empty and meaningless cigarette packet; her 'ethero-topic' delusion had vanished. Through her, the group had to face up to its need to mourn the loss of its pathological solution: delusions. She herself felt like an empty packet all crumpled up. Like some other patients in the group who had found themselves in a fragile state after losing their capacity for delusional thinking, Sandra had tried several times to commit suicide. It was very painful for her when she started to experience feelings again, but in the following session this inspired her to write poetry as she gradually began to 'warm up'. In spite of this, her return to life proved too difficult for her. One weekend, despite the care and attention the staff had for her, she did indeed manage to kill herself.

Sandra's death upset the group tremendously.[3] Their feelings were contra-dictory – some were deeply affected by such a violent and discouraging end, others admired Sandra for her 'courage'. Part of the group turned her into an emblem of death's victory. This defiant narcissistic cathexis of death was very difficult for the staff and for the other group members to integrate. The group's destructive narcissism was working against the constructive forces of the therapeutic process.

Herbert Rosenfeld (1968, 1971) studied destructive narcissism in the psy-chotic transference, which often goes hand in hand with a negative therapeutic reaction. This may emerge in the analysis of psychotic patients who are begin-ning to improve then find themselves facing a new situation with which they cannot cope – for example, a 'catastrophic change' (Bion 1970a). In destructive narcissism, the death drive endeavours to dominate the life drive – and sometimes it succeeds. As Henry Maldiney once said to me: 'The severely depressed patient "dies his life" rather than "lives his death".'

In the session which followed Sandra's suicide, Marco wore a tee-shirt with a picture of a sailing boat on the front. The sail, which the group saw in fantasy as black in colour, took on the appearance of a flag which symbolized both mourning and triumph. Several members of the group stood up and walked around the room as though in a funeral procession. They identified with different parts of the group-boat on Marco's shirt. Giovanni, for example, chose to be an offshore wind, someone else was the sea and the waves, Marco was the tiller – and therefore the captain or charismatic leader of this particular *Ship of Fools* in its state of distress and suffering. Rossana, still silently hiding behind her long hair, unexpectedly took the floor and said: 'I'll be the anchor.' Rossana was fulfilling a very important role for the mad and suicidal boat – the regressive part of the group was thus anchored in the frozen waters of its 'Ice Age'.

Depending on the patient's pathology, there are differences in the 'climate' which presides over depressive states. The psychotic patient's depression is cold and often frozen; the neurotic's is bubbling with anxiety and heat. In this boat scene, these two levels were being fused and confused. Each time the hallucinatory voice of Rossana's mother told her to leave the group, the boat lost its anchor and would begin to bob about in an incoherent and uncoordinated fashion. Rossana was thus an essential part of the group's stability. The group oscillated between life and death, emotional anaesthesia and painful hyperaesthesia, reconciliation and paranoid demands. Tossed about on the waves, we tried to find some possibility of mediation which would help us negotiate these contradictory feelings.

Thus between Eros and Thanatos, positive and negative transference, defiance and gratitude, a complex and difficult confrontation/exchange took place involving the group's antinomic feelings (Gabel 1962). The image of the group boat again reminded me of Bosch's *Ship of Fools*, which I mentioned in Chapter 4. I see in that painting a precursor of what would later become the therapeutic community movement, with its attempt to provide a mental space for madness. In this Tower of Babel, each individual is trying to speak; they can be seen as a number of ideas or thoughts which are in conflict with one another, each one trying to impose its point of view on all the others. Some, however, remain isolated, as though indifferent. A solitary juggler, the group's autistic core, is drinking. Others are deep in the surrounding waters. The mast is a tree, the leaves of which hide a skull – death is present, and demonstrably so. To its trunk is tied a flag waving (dancing) in the wind.

In our group, Sandra represented on the one hand the inability to integrate life and on the other the demise of the delusional solution. The end of the delusion was a deep narcissistic wound which abruptly emerged on the surface of the group's awareness. Coming back to life is a painful process; frozen emotions begin to thaw out – the terrifying shift from mortal anaesthesia to burning liveliness. Panic broke out as they began to wake up. The fear was that the floodwaters would break in a nightmarish way – but if there was danger there was also hope.

During the course of the three years we spent together, there were many changes. Some of the patients left the clinic, others left the group, and there were a few who continued to participate as outpatients. From the point of view of group dynamics, we could say that there were periods of dis-memberment followed by periods of 're-membering'. The latter word also implies that the group was able to recall their past history together as a group. From time to time there was a kind of nostalgia for their ancient Ice Age – 'We didn't even feel the cold then,' they seemed to be saying. In order to feel cold or warm – life – they had first of all to wake up from their frozen state.

Throughout the psychoanalytic and psychotherapeutic process of the group, there were neurotic and psychotic phases, sometimes quite clear-cut, but more often than not combined and mixed together. Regressive processes first of all became less cold then were experienced as more alive and warm. There was always the threat of a catastrophic thaw out, one which would lead to a sort of mental haemorrhage.

One of the problems in psychosis, according to Federn (1953), is the loss of ego boundaries during the psychotic crisis; it then becomes impossible to distinguish between inner and outer space. Freud had already highlighted the loss of the capacity for reality testing and the subsequent absence of feelings of reality in psychosis. Here, the group was at times able to re-establish its boundaries and to repair its internal structure. The group ego thus became a helpful body-ego able to contain the floodwaters of feelings and hold them in check.

In one of her dreams, Silvia, the beautiful Renaissance Madonna, illustrated this theme. She was in an art gallery with her mother; one of them was lying on the floor, wearing a white shirt with 'BIRMANIA' (Burma) written on it in capital letters. Sylvia commented: 'I feel cold'. I understood her to be wakening up from her frozen sleep; she was henceforth able to know what 'cold' meant – 'Brr . . .' as she saw in the dream. And this time it was not 'maniac' (Brr–mania). Silvia's associations and those of some of the group members helped us to understand that the group's frozen mind could be dressed in a tee-shirt/shroud. Their identification with the funeral/funereal tee-shirt meant that they were unable to become a living global unity. When the ego cannot live inside its own boundaries, when it is too painful to be oneself, the ego (or its broken and dismantled fragments) 'escape' and migrate towards other spaces. Each of these fragments expresses a wish or at least the hope of some adventure. They wander off into unexplored, mysterious and exciting places, such as Burma.

In other sessions, this same dream was taken up in situations where Silvia or certain other group members reacted in a manic and dissociated way – a split between depressive and manic feelings or between hot and cold sensations. From time to time, some of these 'fragments' came back into the group, bringing more liveliness – though here again the accompanying anxiety was not always bearable.

The idea of 'fragments of reality' is based on certain of Bion's (1967) ideas on the acute psychotic crisis. I myself have already developed this topic in a seminar in Arles, France, on 'the experience of the object in psychosis' (Resnik 1989). Defying reality can become so powerful that psychotic patients end up attacking their own mental apparatus, which thereupon breaks up into little pieces. The result is severe disorders of perception; sense-data are distorted. When this becomes too difficult to put up with, some of these fragments of reality escape, forming 'wild thoughts'. In the case of our group, the fantasy was that these fragments could live independently – so that the problem then became: how were they to come back home and be reconciled with the other split-off parts of the ego? Moreover, these fragments of reality may be in conflict not only with one another but also with a delusional system. It is the analyst's task to help patients discriminate between these discordant elements. Freud writes:

> mental life is the function of an apparatus to which we ascribe the characteristics of being extended in space and of being made up of several portions

– which we imagine, that is, as resembling a telescope or microscope or something of the kind.

(Freud 1940 [1938]: 145)

The German word *Stucken* (here translated as 'portions') can also mean 'pieces' or 'fragments'.

I suggest that the idea of 'fragments of reality' implies a series of different aspects and functions of a *broken* mental apparatus (rather than a dismantled one). The effect of this is to change the whole landscape of inner and outer reality in a very bizarre way. During the acute catastrophic crisis, each fragment of the broken mental apparatus becomes a confused amalgamation of 'fragments of reality' composed of broken particles of internal objects, fractured links, parts of the ego, visions and landscapes – they make up an apparently incomprehensible jigsaw puzzle of reality.

These fragments are evacuated out of the self through projective identification. The 'success' of this destructive projection appears as a mutilation of the mental apparatus. Bion explains that the expulsion of parts of the ego leads to their independent and uncontrolled existence outside the personality, where they either contain or are contained by external objects.

> Each particle is felt to consist of a real object which is encapsulated in a piece of personality that has engulfed it. The nature of this complete particle will depend partly on the character of the real object, say a gramophone, and partly on the character of the particle of personality that engulfs it. If the piece of personality is concerned with sight, the gramophone when played is felt to be watching the patient; if with hearing, then the gramophone when played is felt to be listening to the patient.
>
> (Bion 1967 [1957]: 39–40)

I find it useful to speak about 'fragments of reality' rather than simply fragments of the mental apparatus, which is nonetheless a complementary notion. If the fragment has to do with a fantasy concerning vegetation, the patient will project it into a vegetable, a vegetable-like object or a tree.

In the group two patients began walking up and down opposite each other, 'cutting' the group in two. They looked like the blades of a pair of scissors – this was a fantasy of cutting links, and was equated with a crucifixion. I have already mentioned the crucifix on the wall of our therapy room; it carries a double message – on the one hand belief and hope, on the other death and being cut off from any other belief.

Lacan's (1971) concept of foreclosure (or repudiation) is interesting here as regards his ideas on psychosis. For Lacan, what is ejected (*Verwerft*) out into the world is what he refers to as 'the name of the father', the paternal metaphor. Thus shut out of the symbolic universe, there is no place for that signifier in the individual's unconscious. According to Lacan, during the psychotic crisis, it is the name of the father which is being rejected, then ejected and enclosed in an external object, and subsequently denied. I suggest that what is being expelled is a broken fragment of inner reality, in which the paternal superego – or a piece of it – is amalgamated with other internal objects and broken parts of the mental apparatus. As a result, a bizarre, extravagant picture of the world is created.

In chronic psychosis, the absence of emotion – 'a-motion' – becomes an ideological, delusional belief; an affirmation in which being almost dead, surrounding oneself with ether, not experiencing life, freezing the affects, etc. is a paradoxical way of coming to terms with existence.

Reintrojection of certain living aspects in the body ego may reawaken fantasies of a 'hypochondriacal body-image' of the group. It is not easy to reintegrate fragments of reality which have been expelled from thinking. Once back in the patient's mental space, they have to be made welcome, but the mental apparatus is not always ready to mentalize the return of these voyagers from afar, these emigrants/immigrants whose return is heavy with anxiety. If the ego cannot cope with the situation, they may be evacuated into the body – this is what I call 'internal projection' into the organs of the body, manifested as hypochondriacal symptoms or by psychosomatic illnesses.

Monica, a patient with very severe hypochondriacal delusions, would often say 'There is something in my mind that drives me crazy. In my anger, I need to get rid of it into my body.' At times, the group would use Monica as a hypochondriacal 'organ' to split off its distressing feelings which were too difficult to mentalize. Monica symbolized the 'somato-psychotic' defensive mechanism for aspects which the group could not resolve mentally. These aspects were materialized in a concrete way through one of the participants – in this case, Monica.

Rossana would use a similar mechanism to 'pour out' her secrets in and into the diaries she kept. She became a sort of priestess-translator or scribe for the hidden and secret messages of the group. She was not only the anchor of the boat-group but also its ink and its ink-stand, the transcriber of its hieroglyphic and enigmatic language. And by turning the anchor upside down to make an inverted cross, she symbolized rebellion against the Christ-image which was so present in the group – the inverted cross is that of the Antichrist. She often spoke about the bomb which the devil had sent her in her role as a witch. In one of her diary notes, she wrote that an inner hallucinated voice had said to her: 'Jesus Christ, you should leave the group.' As though possessed, the 'witch' launched into a long diatribe about '*Resnica*' and '*Res-niet*'; the feminization of my name turned me into a matryoshka-figure for the group, a maternal figure which Rossana tried to disavow by 'negating' me in Russian – '*Res-niet*'.

Thanks to Rossana, the group could express its persecutory and revengeful feelings against the mother-figure (the containing function of the institution). Also, as spokesperson for the group's unconscious, she expressed the group's need for a charismatic leader, a Messiah, the product of a pairing group (Bion) which would lead the group in the proper direction. The task of the 'charismatic' psychoanalyst is to help them reconstruct the fragmented or dismantled mental apparatus of the group ego. Often, envious feelings emerge with respect to the group 'leader' (in the formal sense of the term) and against his (in this case, my) attempts at opening up channels of communication. Repeated attacks against linking can lead to the destruction of the group matrix; we saw this danger in the 'scissors' operation of the two female patients I spoke about earlier.

Marco in his priestly evocation would speak in biblical terms about the Cross, which was his way of helping us to understand that attacks on linking were a sort of repetitive crucifixion. But who was to be crucified? Where was the scapegoat or sacrificial victim? In part, me as the idealized and hated father, and in part the group itself as a maternal body. Envious attacks are directed against any link, any 'bridge', any 'bridging experience' (the father as *'pontifex'* – bridge-builder: see, *passim*, Resnik (1973, 1986) where I indicate that, in Rome, the bridges over the Tiber were a privilege of the Pope or Sovereign Pontiff, who is also a 'bridge' between heaven and earth). I have already mentioned how the psychotic patient attacks the father's linking and structuring function. In the Freudian and Kleinian models, the child attacks the primal scene, just as Rossana attacked the group relationship and that of the combined parents (group–and–therapist).

In his theory of ego nuclei, Glover (1968) suggests that the primitive ego is made up of many parts which manage to become integrated at some point in the development of the individual. The ego's disintegration is the result of the original primary split in the ego. Similarly, we could say that the unbinding, dismantling and demolition typical of the acute psychotic crisis are the fruit of a catastrophic or apocalyptic experience. In a certain sense, the patient 'un-becomes' – losing his or her identity as a sentient being. The therapeutic process of reparation and restoration with psychotic patients could therefore be described as 're-becoming' alive or 're-birth'.

This combination of research and therapy is a difficult task, a necessary one of course, and one that is also fascinating. I have tried to illustrate some relevant points throughout this description of my work with psychotic patients. I am referring here in particular to the transference working-through (*Durcharbeitung*), for which the patient's help is vital. When the patient's infantile ego and that of the analyst wake up, the work of restoration can begin. This reparative aspect can at times be moving when the fragments of the former catastrophe (the precipitating crisis) have to be picked up and brought together. Regression and progression in the psychoanalytic process are alternating phases – the evolution and involution of the transference. The transference is a repetition, a re-presentation of repressed traumatic events. We could think of this in terms of the geology and the ecology of the transference in which the history and the climate of some earlier era is reproduced.

When I was a student, I learned that ontogenesis reproduces phylogenesis. Similarly, in severely regressive states – as in a group of chronic psychotic patients – there is a dramatization of the individual's idea of the mystery of his or her origins. The origins of the Earth, humankind, the cosmos . . . they raise fundamental ontological questions, as philosophers and religions throughout the ages have recognized. The cosmos is a wide screen on to which everything can be projected. I have always been surprised by the fact that the pre-Socratic philosophers spoke so much about 'heavenly bodies' and so little about the ordinary human body. Perhaps Plato's idea of the body-as-prison and the body-as-tomb laid the foundations for some primary anxiety about accepting the physical body as such. In 1957, I was fortunate enough to attend Merleau-Ponty's lectures in the Collège de France on the phenomenology of the body and its relationship to the concept of Nature.

In his geological fantasy, Freud speaks of the individual and his environment as a 'historical precipitate'. As we followed the historical unfolding of the transference, we have seen how this historical precipitate goes through periods of hibernation and thawing out.

Are we able to offer something better than an anaesthetizing hibernation? This kind of question must always be raised, for it helps us to discover the appropriate yardstick of our (let us hope) therapeutic interventions. Thawing out is often experienced as a catastrophic breaking of the floodwaters. Such moments of extreme fragility and distress in a group have to be taken into account and proper care procedures made available to the patients – especially when their delusions have begun to deflate and the question of life or death comes to the fore in all of its acuity. Every therapeutic approach, individual or group, has to respect the 'ethics of the encounter'.

In a treatise on maritime law, I discovered the term 'territorial waters': a country has jurisdiction over a stretch of land, for example, within a certain zone around its coastline, even if the land in question is under water. This indicates the 'identity' of that strip of shore. Perhaps in our unconscious – deep beneath our own 'sea' – there may be zones of this kind which the therapist and the care-giving institution ought always to respect? The idea here would be to establish a relationship with the other person in a way that is not invasive. In psychosis, there are often dramatic instances of intrusion into the patient's private sphere and these may well give cause for a persecutory image of the world. In my book *The Delusional Person* I discuss the focal or ideal distance thanks to which transference communication can be set up in a way which allows all those concerned to preserve their self-identity.

The psychoanalytic process creates a crisis in the false equilibrium of the psychotic world-order; it must therefore propose other alternatives which will enable the patient's world to be reorganized differently.

The work I have described in this chapter – which brought together patients, staff, therapists and observers – represents for me a 'fragment' of the fieldwork research I have been doing for many years now. The experience we shared was one of coexistence. We interacted, sharing our impressions and feelings as regards this slice of life we spent together in the clinic. After the sessions, the observers in the room and on the other side of the mirror met to discuss certain aspects of the institutional and group environment. This enabled us to share a particularly stimulating experience in which each of us was in turn patient and therapist, teacher and pupil.

As regards the role of the therapist and the institutional conditions under which a therapeutic process develops, the work of Stanton and Schwartz (1954) has had an important influence on me. They placed all staff members, whatever their qualifications, on an equal footing – that of participant observers. From my standpoint as an 'apprentice-and-teacher', I would often endeavour to identify the impact that patients' anxieties had on the observer and to sense the way in which they tried to manipulate our mental apparatus. We therefore tried as far as possible to analyse our own conscious and unconscious feelings and reactions with respect not only to the patients in the group but also to a kind of 'psychopathology of everyday life' as it was played out in the context of the clinic as a whole. From a psychoanalytic point of view, I would say that it is essential that we endeavour to make the best possible use of our position as participant observers. This demands a dynamic understanding of the shifts and movements of the institutional transference and counter-transference situation.

## Conclusion

And now we have come to the end of our voyage to the North Pole, where the noise of ancient battles still rings in our ears, and where those 'frozen words' which Pantagruel's 'psychoanalytic spirit' alone could perceive still reverberate.

In Flanders, the actor-painter Hieronymus Bosch expressed the fantastic and dramatic richness of the world of madness in his famous painting *Ship of Fools*. In that work of art, there is not only pathos but also hope. It is the same hope that may emerge in a group of patients. With help, they will be able to make contact with the richness of their delusion and turn it to good use. A delusion is a pathological ideology which all the same has succeeded in preserving certain healthy aspects of the personality; analysis can revive these and launch them on a new voyage.

Every delusion contains a diabolical aspect. In some of Bosch's paintings, the satanic aspect is represented by a monkey. Of that monkey, the purpose of which is to eliminate anything sacred, St Augustine said: 'The devil is the monkey of God', the one whose desire was to 'make a monkey' out of God. In the *Ship of Fools*, hidden in the foliage of the tree-mast, we see the face of a monkey-ghost. One of the 'fools' tries to free himself of the devil by cutting down the trunk which ties him, in his panic and distress, to his diabolical shadow.

The struggle between God and the devil reminds me of William Blake's *Marriage of Heaven and Hell* (1790). In this confrontation, the life and death drives are locked in combat, just like the positive and negative transference.

In Bosch's painting, that struggle is expressed by the monkey-like grimace which belittles the healthy aspects of the personality and opposes every attempt at reconciliation with the principle of reality. In Bosch's work, the predilection for distorting and transforming bodily fantasies corresponds to the creative glimpses the painter had concerning the world of madness. The *Ship of Fools* is, in some ways, a portrait of humanity as a whole. That small society of foolish, nonsensical people sailing down the Rhine cannot but bring to mind that other small group which survived the Flood.

Both the psychotic crisis and the ensuing thawing out reawaken memories of an earlier catastrophic experience – not only of the Flood, but also when Moses was saved from the waters.

Our voyage in company with so-called 'fools' (who, after all, are not so much 'foolish' as sensible-but-suffering individuals who have become aware of the depth of their existential drama) has enabled us to widen their horizons – and, by the same token, our own. The whole point at issue was to help them navigate though the currents and counter-currents of life.

Although Antonin Artaud maintained that life is something that nobody can cure, we *can* help people who have been wounded by life to get in touch with their non-psychotic aspects. They will thus be better prepared to navigate between the inevitable reefs and rocky coasts which life sets in our way.

# 6

# Conclusion

Bringing this book to a close is also a way of writing the concluding chapter to a particularly eventful period of my life. After every 'journey', it is a good idea just to sit down and think things over. For Heraclitus, life is a 'becoming'; but it is also necessary to meditate, to mark a pause in order to take stock of one's situation – simply 'to be', as Parmenides put it.

Most psychoanalytic studies of psychosis – my own included – have focused essentially on the psychotic patient's difficulty as regards his or her thought processes. In this book, I have tried to show – as my own patients have taught me – that schizophrenics are quite capable of thinking . . . in their own way, of course. That is why it is important to endeavour to understand the meaning of their sometimes highly idiosyncratic expressions – their own particular manner of being. In spite of their perhaps discursive and fragmented thinking, their mental and physical mannerisms, such patients are nonetheless able to reconstruct a neo-language which may sound bizarre to our ears. The way in which they express themselves, however, becomes meaningful when we examine it in the appropriate hermeneutic mode. If we learn how to listen carefully to their language and approach it with the intention of getting to know it, it then becomes accessible. Every delusion has its *raison d'être*: this is the logic of the delusion. Bleuler (1911) pointed out that even in the most severe cases of schizophrenia – patients who have lost all contact with the outside world – a universe still exists; it is founded, of course, on the patient's own 'reality' principle and value system. The schizophrenic world is not 'real' in the ordinary sense of the word. Bleuler (1911) used the term *dereistic thinking* in his description of autistic patients. 'Autism' is in fact his invention, though his definition of the condition overlaps to some extent what Freud called 'auto-eroticism' – pleasure has little to do with the real world and thoughts are turned back in on themselves. Geometrically speaking, this could be conceived of as circular thinking – a circle which, at times, may take on the appearance of a halo. The private space of autistic patients, just like the autistic part of schizophrenic

97

patients, is treated as though it were 'sacred ground'. Making contact with such patients may entail a loss of this sacred characteristic – and perhaps even a desecration or profanation.

A patient I have been treating on a regular basis has just told me that he has a halo above his head, made of hallucinated images, voices and smells. A sacred aureole of that kind corresponds to what Frances Tustin (1986) called 'autistic barriers'. The halo transforms my patient into a saint – or into a fallen angel, so downcast is he at times. That is his way of protecting himself (an autistic way, of course) from the surrounding world in which his psychotic dis–illusion has taken root. A delusion is a form of illusion, one which becomes utopian once the delusion itself is deflated. The very word 'delusion' in English highlights this aspect of 'delusive illusion'; in French the term *délire*, with its connotations of undoing or untying, emphasizes the loss of contact with or alienation from ordinary reality. I would point out here that in the transference experience the reality of the delusion is constantly being mixed in with that of everyday normality.

The most difficult task which the therapist/participant observer has to accomplish is that of acting as mediator (in the transference) between two types of reality: the one which corresponds to the patient's 'psychotic culture', and the normative reality as personified by the analyst. This, then, is a confrontation between realities and between principles – psychotics, too, want to hold on to their principles.

I have often been fascinated, in individual as well as in group sessions, by the complex and evocative nature of psychotic reality. When I look at the groups of psychotic patients I have treated, I realize just what is really meant by under-standing the discourse of the unconscious (which, as Lacan (1971) said, is structured like a language). The reality of the transference between patients takes on the features of a specific linguistic culture. Inside the 'halo', the autistic language exists alongside its schizophrenic counterpart. From time to time, the halo becomes porous, permeable – that is when I can make contact with the patients' world just as they make contact with mine.

Life is an unpredictable journey on the theatre-stage of the world. The psychoanalytic experience of psychosis is, in my view, an absorbing linguistic and cultural adventure. From time to time the situation can be disturbing. Writing of the unusual aspects of our existence, Freud used the term 'uncanny' to describe these unknown yet somehow familiar features. To embark on an adventure can be both gruelling and stimulating. The quest for the unknown leads us off the beaten track into unfamiliar territory; when we leave a well-trodden path, we may well find ourselves in a forest which is as magical as it is terrifying. To do this, we have to leave our everyday routine behind us and put up with some degree of 'exciting' insecurity. Routine is a model of security for which the price to pay is boredom; it takes us along roads which are already familiar to us, where there is little risk of losing our way.

Routine, with its connotations of route, evokes for me the idea of road or highway. If we lose our way, we are thrown off course as it were – and this is where the adventure begins, this is where we have to be capable of carrying out our wish to follow our own path through the forest.

Following the psychotic transference is one way of letting ourselves lose our bearings in order to wander through unfamiliar territory. I often lose my way in the company of a psychotic patient – we are together in the adventure; as I gradually learn more about his or her secret and sacred reality, I can have access to it little by little. Opening oneself up to the reality of the other person is a way of leaving the well-trodden paths of one's 'familiar' life. Such a journey would be a study of the hidden, enigmatic aspects of existence.

Trying to understand psychosis makes us face up to our own existence and sense of reality. In the dynamics of the transference, we become aware of our own unconscious labyrinthine pathways. Between normality and pathology the repressed conflicts of our travels through life, through the time (history) or space of our body and of Nature, are revealed. In this way, new possibilities of travel open up within the psychoanalytic experience.

Working-through (*Durcharbeitung*) – or, as I would put it, the work of the transference – provides us with a learning process which will help us create an image in our mind of how the therapy is operating. What I am trying to transmit in my approach to psychosis is the importance for the analyst to be authentic and for the work of the analysis to be similarly so: the 'style' appropriate to each of us.

This book does not pretend to teach the reader how to psychoanalyse psychotic patients. It simply narrates 'my' way of doing things, my manner of being in the analytical experience. In my view, every analyst must develop his or her own technique. Psychotic patients are very sensitive to the 'originality' – the sincerity – of other people. Being natural and spontaneous – whatever the doubts which may remain in one's head – can be a major contribution to the success of the treatment; imitating someone else's style may well prove iatrogenic.

When I was in supervision with Bion, I remember his saying: 'If we happen to make a mistake during a session, it's not really so important; being relaxed and spontaneous – being oneself – is really what it's all about.' The work of an analysis becomes truly creative when, over and beyond the prescribed or preordained technique, we manage to introduce something of a *tekhné* – one's own crafts-manship and art.

The reality of the psychoanalytic experience, the fieldwork of the analysis, is simultaneously research and therapy. Freud often quoted Pierre Janet on the function of reality – Freud himself, of course, emphasized the fact that the reality principle always comes up against the other person's reality. Reality (*Wirklich*) contains a reference to what is factual. According to Kant (1896), what is perceptible is the phenomenological reality of something, not its inner reality or essence – the *noumena*. The *noumena* or thing-in-itself is not directly knowable through the senses. Kant spoke of several types of reality, including objective reality and empirical reality. In Latin, *realitas* signifies the true qualities of the *res*, the thing. In the idea of reality (*Wirklichkeit*), there is a reference to *Wirkung* and the verb *wirken* – to move or to act. Once again we have the notion of movement, movement of the body as a feature of life itself. With schizophrenic patients, the transference is often devitalized and immobile; in chronic conditions, affects are often frozen or congealed, feelings are iced over. That is why it is important, 'after the Flood', to reawaken movement (*wirken*) and establish a new rhythm of life in the transference.

I hope the reader will have discovered, in these *Glacial Times*, the meaning of the quest I began – the journey I set out on – in the early 1950s. The adventure still fascinates me. The aesthetic travels which have marked my approach to psychosis are still very much part of my activity now – and I have lost, I trust, none of my enthusiasm, none of my warmth in the process. I have tried in this book to communicate some of my thoughts and hypotheses, with the hope that the reader will be able to dialogue mindfully not only with me but also with his or her own feelings and motivations.

# Notes

## Preface

1   These lectures were published in issues 9 and 10 of *L'Information Psychiatrique*, a review available only to subscribers.
2   It is important to distinguish between Bion's (1970a) concept of catastrophic change and Kurt Goldstein's (1848: 13) idea of 'catastrophic conditions' – the event that precipitates the onset of a psychotic breakdown.

## Chapter 1

1   Antoine Destutt de Tracy (1754–1836), a French philosopher and pupil of Condillac, was an encyclopaedist who instigated the Ideologists' Groups. He was the first to introduce the word 'ideology', defining it as the science of ideas, their nature, their laws, their relationship with the signs that represent them and, above all, their origin. Destutt de Tracy's concept helped me to take a fresh look at delusions: a more or less systematized idea system in which the ideas themselves are in conflict with one another as well as with society at large. That kind of inter-necine struggle may perhaps be contained by petrification or by glaciation, as I shall demonstrate later. From a sociological point of view, Destutt de Tracy's ideas were taken up by, among others, Louis Althusser.
2   My use of the word transference in the sense of transmission is due to Jacques Lardaud, who brought to my attention the remarkable work done by Dr Barande (personal communication).
3   Freud's paper, written in 1915, was discovered in 1983. It is a metapsychological text which was thought lost or destroyed – and as such now has the essential quality of having been exhumed or unearthed: 'an exquisite corpse', a surrealistic *cadavre exquis*.

### Chapter 3

1   Though Raul Usandivaras and I (Juan Morgan was not yet one of the co-therapists) were co-therapists, we had decided that it would be upsetting for the patients if both of us were to make comments, interpretations, etc. It seemed crucial that we be clearly distinguishable one from the other: one of us would comment and interpret, while the other would remain silent and take notes. I have always found it preferable to have a single analyst, with any co-workers as silent observers. For unconscious reasons, groups will tend to reproduce the Oedipal pattern of attacking links, dividing the 'parents', and creating conflicts within the parental couple.

### Chapter 4

1   An earlier version of this chapter with the title 'The Space of Madness' appeared in Pines (1985).
2   In French the verb *voler* means both 'to fly' and 'to steal' – a phonetic equation in which the same word carries two different meanings. Compare also Freud's remarks on 'le premier vol de l'Aigle' ('the Eagle's first flight'), in *Jokes and their Relation to the Unconscious* (Freud 1905a: 37).

### Chapter 5

1   An earlier version of this chapter with the title 'Glacial Times in Psychotic Regression' appeared in Schermer and Pines (1994).
2   © the Samuel Beckett Estate and the Calder Educational Trust, 2004.
3   I am grateful for the comments made by Dr Chris Evans in his review of the original version of this chapter (Evans 1996).

# Bibliography

Artaud, A. (1938). *Théâtre et son Double. The Theatre and its Double*, trans. V. Corti. London: Calder & Boyars 1970.

Beckett, S. (1965). *Imagination Dead Imagine*. London: Calder & Boyars.

Bergson, H. (1939). *Matière et Mémoire*. In Bergson, H. (1970) *Œuvres*. Paris: Presses Universitaires de France.

Bion, W. R. (1956). 'The Development of Schizophrenic Thought'. *International Journal of Psycho-Analysis*, **37**: 344–346. Also in Bion, W. R. (1967). *Second Thoughts*. London: Heinemann. Reprinted London: Karnac 1984.

Bion, W. R. (1957). 'The Differentiation of the Psychotic from the Non-psychotic Personalities'. *International Journal of Psycho-Analysis*, **38**: 266–275. Also in Bion, W. R. (1967). *Second Thoughts*. London: Heinemann. Reprinted London: Karnac 1984.

Bion, W. R. (1959). 'Attacks on Linking'. *International Journal of Psycho-Analysis*, **40**: 305–315. Also in Bion, W. R. (1967). *Second Thoughts*. London: Heinemann. Reprinted London: Karnac 1984.

Bion, W. R. (1961). *Experiences in Groups*. London: Tavistock. Reprinted London: Routledge 1991.

Bion, W. R. (1967). *Second Thoughts*. London: Heinemann. Reprinted London: Karnac 1984.

Bion, W. R. (1970a). *Attention and Interpretation*. London: Tavistock. Reprinted London: Karnac 1984. Reprinted in Bion, W. R. (1977). *Seven Servants*. New York: Jason Aronson.

Bion, W. R. (1970b). 'The Mystic and the Group'. In Bion, W. R. (1970). *Attention and Interpretation*. London: Karnac.

Bion, W. R. (1977). 'Emotional Turbulence'. In Bion, W. R. (1977). *Borderline Personality Disorders*. New York: International Universities Press. Reprinted in Bion, W. R. (1987). *Clinical Seminars and Four Papers*, ed. F. Bion. Abingdon: Fleetwood Press. Also in Bion, W. R. (1994). *Clinical Seminars and Other Works*. London: Karnac.

Bion, W. R. (1978). *Four Discussions with W. R. Bion*. Strath Tay, Scotland: Clunie Press. Reprinted in Bion, W. R. (1994) *Clinical Seminars and Other Works*. London: Karnac.

Blake, W. (1975 [1790]). *The Marriage of Heaven and Hell*. Oxford: Oxford University Press.

Bleuler, E. (1911). *Dementia Praecox oder die Gruppe der Schizofrenien*. In Aschaffenburg, G. (ed.) *Handbuch der Psychiatrie*. Leipzig and Vienna. *Dementia Praecox or the Group of Schizophrenias*, trans. J. Zinkin. New York: International Universities Press 1950.

Bria, P and de Risio, S. (1992). 'Vicissitudes de la pensée dans les groupes'. *Revue de Psychothérapie Psychanalytique*, **18**: 25–38.

Carrington, L. (1994) 'Down Below'. In *VVV* (New York), **4** (February): 70–86. Also in Carrington, L. (1990). *The House of Fear: Notes from Down Below*. New York: Penguin.

Dante, A. (1943 [*c*. 1307]) *The Divine Comedy*. London: Dent (Temple Classics).

Descartes, R. (1638). 'A Reneri pour Pollot'. In Descartes, R. (1954). *Lettres*. Textes choisis par M. Alexandre. Paris: Presses Universitaires de France.

Devereux, G. (1967). *From Anxiety to Method in the Behavioral Sciences*. The Hague: Mouton.

Durkheim, E. (1895). *Les Règles de la Méthode Sociologique*. Paris: Alcan. *The Rules of Sociological Method*, trans. S. A. Solovay and J. H. Mueller. Chicago: University of Chicago Press. Edited with Introduction by G. E. G. Catlin. Republished Glencoe, Ill.: Free Press of Glencoe 1950. Also in Lukes, S. (ed.) (1982). *The Rules of Sociological Method and Selected Texts on Sociology and its Method*, trans. W. D. Halls. New York: Free Press.

Evans, C. (1996). 'Review of Schermer, V. L. and Pines, M. (eds) (1994). *Ring of Fire: Primitive Affects and Object Relations in Group Psychotherapy*'. *British Journal of Psychotherapy*, **12**(4): 532–535.

Ezriel, H. (1950). 'A Psycho-analytic Approach to Group Therapy'. *British Journal of Medical Psychology*, **23**: 59–74.

Federn, P. (1953). *Ego Psychology and the Psychoses*, ed. E. Weiss. New York: Basic Books; London: Imago.

Fenichel, O. (1953). 'Respiratory Introjection'. In *The Collected Papers of Otto Fenichel, first series*. New York: Norton.

Ferenczi, S. (1909). 'Introjection and Transference'. In Ferenczi, S. (1952). *First Contributions to Psycho-Analysis*. London: Hogarth. Reprinted London: Maresfield Reprints 1980.

Foulkes, S. H. (1964). *Therapeutic Group Analysis*. London: Allen & Unwin; New York: International Universities Press.

Freud, S. (1894). 'The Neuro-Psychoses of Defence'. *Standard Edition*, **3**: 41–61.

Freud, S. (1896). 'Further Remarks on the Neuro-Psychoses of Defence'. *Standard Edition*, **3**: 162–185.

Freud, S. (1898). 'Sexuality in the Aetiology of the Neuroses'. *Standard Edition*, **3**: 259–285.

Freud, S. (1900). *The Interpretation of Dreams. Standard Edition*, **4–5**.

Freud, S. (1905a). *Jokes and their Relation to the Unconscious. Standard Edition*, **8**.

Freud, S. (1905b). *Three Essays on the Theory of Sexuality. Standard Edition*, **7**: 123–243.

Freud, S. (1906). 'My Views on the Part played by Sexuality in the Aetiology of the Neuroses'. *Standard Edition*, **7**: 271.

Freud, S. (1911). 'Psycho-Analytic Notes on an Autobiographical Account of a Case of Paranoia (Dementia Paranoides)'. *Standard Edition*, **12**: 1–79.

Freud, S. (1917 [1915]). 'Mourning and Melancholia'. *Standard Edition*, **14**: 237–258.

Freud, S. (1919). 'The "Uncanny"'. *Standard Edition*, **17**: 217–252.

Freud, S. (1921). *Group Psychology and the Analysis of the Ego. Standard Edition*, **18**: 65–143.

Freud, S. (1923). *The Ego and the Id. Standard Edition*, **19**: 1–59.

Freud, S. (1933 [1932]). *New Introductory Lectures on Psycho-Analysis. Standard Edition*, **22**: 1–182.

Freud, S. (1940 [1938]). *An Outline of Psycho-Analysis. Standard Edition*, **23**: 139–207.

Freud, S. (1985 [1915]). *A Phylogenetic Fantasy: An Overview of the Transference Neuroses*, ed. I. Grubrich-Simitis; trans. A. and P. T. Hoffer. Cambridge, Mass.: Harvard University Press.

Gabel, J. (1962). *La Fausse Conscience*. Paris: Editions de Minuit.

Glover, E. (1968). *The Birth of the Ego*. New York: International Universities Press; London: George Allen & Unwin.

Goethe, J. W. von (1978 [1809]). *Elective Affinities*, trans. J. Hollingdale. London: Penguin Classics. Reprinted Oxford: Oxford University Press 1999.

Goldstein, K. (1963 [1939]) *The Organism: A Holistic Approach to Biology Derived from Pathological Data in Man*. New York: American Book Company.

Goldstein, K. (1948). *Language and Language Disturbances*. New York: Grune & Stratton.

Griesinger, W. (1882). *Mental Pathology and Therapeutics*, trans. C. Lockhart Robertson and J. Rutherford, 2nd edn. New York: William Wood.

Heidegger, M. (1962 [1927]). *Sein und Zeit. Being and Time*, trans. J. Macquarrie and E. Robinson. New York: Harper & Row.

Heimann, P. (1942). *About Children and Children-No-Longer*, ed. M. Tonnesmann. London: Routledge.

Isaacs, S. (1952). 'The Nature and Function of Phantasy'. In Klein, M., Heimann, P., Isaacs, S. and Riviere, J. (1952). *Developments in Psycho-Analysis*. London: Hogarth Press.

Jacques, E. (1955). 'Social Systems as a Defence against Persecutory and Depressive Anxiety'. In Klein, M., Heimann, P. and Money-Kyrle, R. (eds) *New Directions in Psycho-Analysis*. London: Tavistock. Reprinted London: Karnac 1985.

Kaës, R. (1993). *Le Groupe et le Sujet du Groupe*. Paris: Dunod.

Kant, I. (1963 [1896]). *Critique of Pure Reason*, trans. N. K. Smith 1929. London: Macmillan.

Kardiner, A. (1945). 'The Concept of Basic Personality Structure as an Operational Tool in the Social Sciences'. In Linton, R. (ed.), *The Science of Man in the World Crisis*. New York: Columbia University Press.

King, P. and Steiner, R. (eds) (1991). *The Freud–Klein Controversies 1941–45*. London: Routledge.

Klein, M. (1930). 'The Importance of Symbol-Formation in the Development of the Ego'. *International Journal of Psycho-Analysis*, **11**: 24–39. Also in Klein, M. (1975). *Love, Guilt and Reparation: The Writings of Melanie Klein*, vol. 1. London: Hogarth Press. Reprinted London: Karnac and the Institute of Psycho-Analysis 1992.

Klein, M. (1940). 'Mourning and its Relation to Manic-Depressive States'. *International Journal of Psycho-Analysis*, **21**: 125–153. Also in Klein, M. (1975). *Love, Guilt and*

*Reparation: The Writings of Melanie Klein*, vol. 1. London: Hogarth Press. Reprinted London: Karnac and the Institute of Psycho-Analysis 1992.

Klein, M. (1952). 'The Origins of Transference'. *International Journal of Psycho-Analysis*, **33**: 433–438. Also in Klein, M. (1975). *Envy and Gratitude: The Writings of Melanie Klein*, vol. 3. London: Hogarth Press. Reprinted London: Karnac and the Institute of Psycho-Analysis 1993.

Lacan, J. (1971). *Ecrits II*. Paris: Editions du Seuil.

Laing, R. D. (1960). *The Divided Self: A Study of Sanity and Madness*. London: Tavistock.

Lavater, J-K. (1979 [1775–1778]). *La Physiognomonie ou l'art de connaître les hommes*. Lausanne, Switzerland: L'Age d'Homme.

Lewin, K. (1963 [1951]). *Field Theory in Social Science: Selected Theoretical Papers*, ed. D. Cartwright. New York: Harper & Row; London: Tavistock.

Matte-Blanco, I. (1975). *The Unconscious as Infinite Sets: An Essay in Bi-logic*. London: Duckworth. Revised edn, London: Karnac 1998.

Minkowski, E. (1927). *La Schizophrénie*. Paris: Payot.

Money-Kyrle, R. (1978). *The Collected Papers of Roger Money-Kyrle*, ed. D. Meltzer. Strath Tay, Scotland: Clunie Press.

Nietzsche, F. (1969 [1883]). *Thus Spoke Zarathustra*, trans. R. J. Hollingdale. Harmondsworth: Penguin.

Pichon-Rivière, E. (1947). 'Psicoanalisis de la Esquizofrenia'. *Revista de Psicoanalisis*, **2** (November–December): 293–304.

Pines, M. (1978). 'Group Analytic Psychotherapy of the Borderline Patient'. *Group Analysis*, **11**: 115–126.

Pines, M. (ed.) (1985). *Bion and Group Psychotherapy*. London and Boston, Mass.: Routledge. Reprinted London: Jessica Kingsley 2000.

Rabelais, F. (1955 [1532–1562]). *Gargantua and Pantagruel: The Histories of Gargantua and Pantagruel*, trans. J. M. Cohen. Harmondsworth: Penguin.

Resnik, S. (1971). 'L'Enfant qui habite chez l'adulte'. Unpublished conference paper read before the Milan Psychoanalytic Institute.

Resnik, S. (1973). *Personne et Psychose*. Paris: Payot, 2nd edn Larmor-Plage: Editions du Hublot 1999. *The Delusional Person: Bodily Feelings in Psychosis*, trans. D. Alcorn. London: Karnac 2001.

Resnik, S. (1980). 'A Propos de la dépression narcissique'. In *Regard, accueil et présence: Mélanges en l'honneur de Georges Daumézon*. Toulouse: Privat.

Resnik, S. (1984). 'La Grimace d'Akhenaton'. In *Cahiers de psychologie de l'art et de la culture*, **10**: 123. Paris: Editions de l'Ecole Nationale Supérieure des Beaux-Arts.

Resnik, S. (1985a). 'The Psychotic Crisis'. *British Journal of Psychotherapy*, **2**(1): 5–19.

Resnik, S. (1985b). 'The Space of Madness'. In Pines, M. (ed.). *Bion and Group Psychotherapy*. London and Boston, Mass.: Routledge.

Resnik, S. (1986). *L'Esperienza Psicotica*. Turin: Bollati Boringhieri.

Resnik, S. (1988). 'Psychose et Institution', in *A Clinical Journey*, vol. 1 of 5 vols. A Collection of Salomon Resnik's 'Writings', privately published by the Cultural Association of the Alès Hospital, in the Cévennes, France.

Resnik, S. (1989). 'Fragments de Réalité'. In Chouvier, B., Dimier, C., Gimenez, G., Granjon, E., Guérin, C., Du Lac, M., Paul, S., Resnik, S., Thaon, M. and Vidal, J. P., *L'Expérience de l'Objet dans la Psychose. Actes des Journées d'Etude de Psychologie*

*Sociale et Clinique* organisées par le C.O.R., Hôpital Joseph Imbert, Arles, February 1989: 43–50.

Resnik, S. (1990). *Spazio Mentale*. Turin: Bollati Boringhieri. *Mental Space*, trans. D. Alcorn. London: Karnac 1995.

Resnik, S. (1993). *Lo Fantástico en lo Cotidiano*. Madrid: Julián Yébenes.

Resnik, S. (2001a). 'Seminario di Bion a Parigi'. *Koinos*, **22**(1–2): 9–37.

Resnik, S. (2001b). 'Bodily Feelings in a Dreaming World'. IPA Congress, Nice (France) 2001. *Archives of Psychiatry and Psychotherapy*, **6**(1): 45–53.

Resnik, S., Antonetti, A. and Ficacci, M-A. (1982). *Semiologia dell'incontro*. Rome: Il Pensiero Scientifico.

Rolland, R. (1918). *Empedocle d'Agrigente*. Paris: Albin Michel 2000.

Rosenfeld, H. A. (1968). 'Negative Therapeutic Reaction'. *Scientific Bulletin of the British Psycho-Analytical Society*, **133**. Also in Giovacchini, P. (ed.) (1975). *Tactics and Techniques in Psycho-Analytic Therapy*, vol. 2. London: Hogarth Press.

Rosenfeld, H. (1971). 'A Clinical Approach to the Psychoanalytic Theory of the Life and Death Instincts: An Investigation into the Aggressive Aspects of Narcissism'. *International Journal of Psycho-Analysis*, **52**: 169–178.

Schermer, V. L. and Pines, M. (eds) (1994). *Ring of Fire: Primitive Affects and Object Relations in Group Psychotherapy*. London: Routledge.

Schilder, P. (1939). 'Results and Problems of Group Psychotherapy in Severe Neuroses'. *Review of Mental Hygiene* (New York), **23**: 87–98.

Schilder, P. (1950). *The Image and Appearance of the Human Body*. New York: International Universities Press. Reprinted London: Routledge 1999.

Segal, H. (1957). 'Notes on Symbol Formation'. *International Journal of Psycho-Analysis*, **38**: 391–397. Also in *The Work of Hanna Segal*. New York: Jason Aronson, 1981.

Stanton, A. H. and Schwartz, M. S. (1954). *The Mental Hospital: A Study of Institutional Participation in Psychiatric Illness and Treatment*. New York: Basic Books.

Tustin, F. (1986). *Autistic Barriers in Neurotic Patients*. New Haven, Conn.: Yale University Press; London: Karnac.

Wellisch, E. (1954). *Isaac and Oedipus: A Study in Biblical Psychology of the Sacrifice of Isaac, The Akedah*. London: Routledge & Kegan Paul.

Von Hartmann, E. (1931 [1868]). *Philosophy of the Unconscious: Speculative Results According to the Inductive Method of Physical Science*, trans. W. C. Coupland. London: Kegan Paul, Trench, Trübner; New York: Harcourt, Brace.

Von Uexkull, J. (1920). *Theoretische Biologie*. Berlin. *Theoretical Biology*. London: Kegan Paul, Trench, Trübner 1926.

# Name index

Abraham, 31–2, 34
Ardenquin, 14
Aristotle, 42, 51, 53–4, 71
Artaud, 5, 96

Balint, 19
Beckett, 70, 71
Berg, 17
Bion, 7, 9, 16, 23, 40, 41, 43, 55, 56, 60, 62, 72, 77, 78, 80, 88, 90, 91, 93, 99
Blake, 96
Bosch, 60, 72, 89, 95–6

Cotard, 22

Daumézon, 52
De Chirico, 77
Descartes, 13, 42
Destutt de Tracy, 4
Devereux, 72
Dilthey, 21
Durkheim, 6

Empedocles of Agrigente, 20
Evans, 102 (*note 2 to Chapter 5*)
Ezriel, 15

Federn, 16, 90
Fenichel, 13
Ferlini, 71, 74, 78, 86, 87
Ficin, 3
Flechsig, 5

Foulkes, 44
Freud, 2, 3, 5, 7, 8, 12, 15, 16–17, 19, 23–4, 26, 63, 67, 71, 72, 77, 78, 81, 82, 83, 86, 90, 93, 94, 97, 98, 99–100

Gabel, 89
Glover, 60, 93
Goldstein, 8
Griesinger, 26, 81

Hegel, 6, 21
Heidegger, 20, 57
Heimann, 23

Kant, 99, 100
Klein, 2, 8, 14, 16, 23, 24, 25, 26, 30, 48, 72, 81, 83, 85
Koffka, 9
Kohler, 9
Krapf, 40

Lacan, 7, 23, 91–2, 98
Lardaud, 101n
Lavater, 5
Leibovitz, 17
Lewin, 9

Magritte, 27
Maldiney, 88
Matte-Blanco, 7
Merleau-Ponty, 94

# Subject index

a-motion, 92
anxiety, 12, 13, 23, 36, 38, 45, 46, 48,
  49, 50, 57, 72, 73, 76, 77, 78, 80, 85,
  87, 88, 90, 92, 94; psychotic anxiety,
  46, 72, 84
apocalypse, 59, 68
autism, 51, 97

Burma, 90
body language, 5, 42, 44, 47, 71
borderline, 84

catastrophic change, 79, 88, 101n2
catastrophic experience, 15, 26, 60, 86,
  96, 101n2
communication, 11, 12, 41, 43, 44, 72,
  79, 82, 93, 94
confusion, 27
counter-transference, 4, 11, 13, 15, 18,
  42, 47, 51, 60, 72, 95

deflation, 33, 69, 75, 80, 86, 87
delusion, delusional, 4–5, 6, 19, 25, 27,
  29, 30, 32, 33–5, 48, 56, 58, 59, 60,
  62–7, 68, 69, 72, 73, 77–8, 80, 86,
  87–8, 89, 90, 92, 94, 95, 97–8
depersonalization, 16–17, 46
depression, 12, 26, 56, 74, 77, 88; basic
  depression, 26, 81; narcissistic
  depression, 4, 29, 33, 67, 75, 86, 87
derealization, 17
dis-illusion, 4, 69, 86, 98

dis-membering, 62
dissociation, 4, 17, 42, 46, 47, 85
distance, 29, 51, 82, 83, 94
double transference, 11, 51
*Durcharbeitung*, 69, 93, 99

ecology of the transference, 39, 93
ego ideal, 4, 23, 29, 33, 75, 84, 86
emotion, 31–3, 36–7, 46, 59–60, 62,
  64, 66, 68–9, 75, 78, 80–81, 85, 89,
  92
'e-motion', 55, 75
emptiness, 25, 46–7, 65, 70, 71, 74, 78,
  82, 85

false self, 23
field, 9, 12–13, 67, 71, 94, 99
flood, 77, 79, 82, 89–90, 94, 96, 100
fragment of reality, 84, 90–92
folly, 33, 75, 76
foreclosure (*forclusion*), 91
freezing and de-freezing (thawing-out),
  19, 26, 33, 35–6, 38, 39, 40, 43, 45,
  53, 55, 58, 60, 63, 66, 68–9, 77, 79,
  82, 85, 89, 92, 94, 96
frozen words, 52, 54, 95

group matrix, 44, 62, 63, 93
group self, 55, 56, 58, 62, 80, 85

hallucinate, hallucination, 19, 24, 27, 41,
  72, 76, 82, 87, 89, 92, 98

111